THISday

MODERN ESSAYS OF ENLIGHTENMENT

WORDS FOR THE VULNERABLE
AND THE VENERABLE

PHILIP GABBARD

THISday

Words for the Vulnerable and the Venerable

Published by Wheatmark®
2030 East Speedway Boulevard, Suite 106
Tucson, Arizona 85719 USA
www.wheatmark.com

ISBN: 978-1-62787-781-7
LCCN: 2019915546

Bulk ordering discounts are available through Wheatmark, Inc. For more information, email orders@wheatmark.com or call 1-888-934-0888.

My Gratitude

If you know me, then thank you, for as you shall see, you are woven into the fabric of every word of *THISday*. To my wife, Gaby, and my children, Hannah, Greyson, and Isaak, who embody THISlove of which I must speak. And to Mom and Dad, *y mi familia*: You Are the Heart of *THISday*.

To all to my partners, teammates, coaches, customers, and friends: You are my blessings counted THISday and every day, and without you my days would be unfulfilled. And thanks be to God; for THESEdays and THESEwords for which we are about to share. Amen.

Mil Gracias, por todo.

Foreword
by Jack B. Rochester

Poets, singers, and storytellers from every walk of life have long admonished us to live for today. Scientists, philosophers, novelists, musicians, spiritualists, one and all, have counseled us that we can't change the past and the future is unknown, so we should just concentrate on living today to the best of our ability.

Now, Philip Gabbard has written *THISday*, a book of, by, and for the Everyman in all of us. Gabbard's book is the story of his unintentional path of grappling with life's conflicts and the resulting understanding and enlightenment. It's not a path that he set out to take because, like most of us, he roamed about, followed the ways of the human herd for a while, wandered away, got lost, questioned where he was going—even why he was on the path. Any path. He wondered how he was expected to understand his past experiences and focus them to learn how to get to something or somewhere in the future. Why were there societal rules and expectations? Who made them? Why so many shoulds, have-tos, mantras, which demanded conformity?

But Gabbard began questioning these conventional expectations, scarcely realizing the many outcomes his challenges to rote behaviors would have on him. He soon learned that he needed to unlearn a lot of what he had been taught, including these expectations. But in doing so, he learned he would expose himself to a great deal of misunderstanding, criticism, and even rejection.

Undaunted, Gabbard came to realize that figuring this stuff out had been, and would become, his lifelong occupation. It was not the destination; it was the journey itself, undertaken one day at a time.

What it took was simple: All he had to do was just show up and take good care of the journey and the people, places and events along the way. This collection of intimate, revealing, intensely personal essays portray how Everyman Philip Gabbard learned to show up for THISday—and for himself. And in doing so, his goal became writing about his journey and inspiring others to find and explore their own path.

Michel de Montaigne, the world's first personal essayist, wrote, "The greatest thing in the world is to know how to belong to oneself." Philip Gabbard would concede this is no simple task, yet each and every one of us possesses the raw materials from which to shape ourselves into exactly who and what we wish to be. That requires letting go of the past and all its baggage: fear, loss, doubt, remorse, shame, mistakes, pain. It demands our accepting that we have no knowledge, nor a prescribed *way*, into the future. Tomorrow is the great unknown, and although some would tempt us with their clever insurance policies for a glorious—or, on the other hand, warn us of a possibly insufferable—afterlife, it is meaningless unless we live today to the very best of our ability. As soon as we bring that objective into clear focus, we can begin to live a rich and meaningful today, not just for ourselves but for all of those we know and love.

Learning to unlearn the conformity traps that face each of us and shifting his perspective accordingly, Gabbard finds himself in pursuit of a more mindful path. With clearer thoughts built from a new construct of words and meanings, he—and we—can experience deep, profound, lasting change and have better moments, days, weeks, months, and years—one day at a time.

THISday is not a how-to or advice book. Nor is it a self-help treatise, except in the sense that Gabbard, like Montaigne, writes of learning to help himself through the lenses of perspective and passionate pursuit of understanding. Woven into Gabbard's tapestry of tales of his satori are the means by which he achieved his enlightenment. He tells us about these in plain speak, and yet because these are simple tales, they may be overlooked by the casual reader who is not receptive or is not in true pursuit of understanding. But Gabbard does not soft-pedal for the weak at heart. Instead, he tells a new story, then another and another. They are the stories an awakening higher consciousness.

The first tool is words. Gabbard understands how words define and shape everything we do, impact every sensory perception, and determine every outcome. He knows that choosing, as the French say, *le mot juste* can make all the difference in the quality of human interactions.

Gabbard ponders how words are evoked from both external as well as internal sources. Words, spoken or thought, lead to more thoughts, which in turn guide our beliefs, actions, personal growth, and life experiences. Our best experiences occur today, and only today, *by our choice*; not by luck, destiny, or the favor of the universe; not even by prayer. Our choices are the linchpins to lifelong happiness and success, self-empowerment, meaningful personal and professional relationships, self-discovery, overcoming depression, and personal breakthroughs. Our choices are predicated on our thoughts, feelings, and beliefs, and they are always built from words. Get the words right, and you get the right thoughts, feelings, beliefs, actions. Get them wrong, disaster.

And as Gabbard comes to this knowledge, he realizes that living a rewarding and meaningful life is only possible by focusing on life as it is today. By choosing this sharp, well-defined, narrow focus—ignoring the effluvia of yesterday and the pointless wondering about tomorrow—his consciousness grows and rises to ever higher levels. He calls this *perception*, and he discusses it often. Gabbard's message is succinct and on point: elevating our awareness, our consciousness, our understanding of ourselves as complex beings, and learning how to fully and honestly express ourselves (and our humanity) are the greatest experiences we can have. All it requires is embracing personal change and centering ourselves in THISday. Achieving this, we are naturally compelled to offer and share this gift with others.

Because change is the prerequisite, we must open up ourselves to challenge the aforementioned assumptions, beliefs, habits, attitudes. Gabbard expresses this as allowing ourselves to be *vulnerable*. He describes the internal battle with the ego to break through to the other side of all the egoistic ramparts we have constructed for ourselves. In the pages of *THISday*, he shows us how he confronts and conquers ego and emerges a better person. *THISday* is an adventure into exposing our vulnerabilities and, once conquered, emerging as a braver individual. This bravery is found in the truest words: speaking or writing what needs to be said, when it needs to be said.

In other words, *THISday* evokes a newfound bravery with our words, our communication within our consciousness of mind, mouth, and moment. When we are stopped, shut down, afraid, insecure, or otherwise held back from doing and saying what needs to be said and done, bravery must rise and prevail. When our thoughts, beliefs, words—most of them learned from timeworn social norms—throw up barriers, we will need new thoughts, new words, new actions, and a large dose of bravery to break through to a higher consciousness.

This is no simple or onetime task. It requires patience and diligence and learning how to break free of our preconceived notions and past behaviors. Achieving higher consciousness is a hard-won gift. It is its own reward for our bravery; only we ourselves know what it took to achieve. And it isn't for everyone, any more than climbing Everest is. But Philip Gabbard did it, and he wants you to know how it went for him. His stories in *THISday* provide the impetus, the experience, and the courage for the pursuit of becoming a braver, truer, more enlightened human being and the promise of the best THISdays of our lives.

Contents

Really? You want a table of contents?

Let me introduce you to what you are about to read, for it has no table of contents.

Like life, there is only what we write into the middle pages that adds content and contentment to our story. That is what I have done here. Like life, it's random; there is a beginning and an end, what happens in between is simply chunks of experience, phantom fears, choice. But fear no more suffering, and suffer no more from your fear of conformity, as you will likely survive this day. *THISday*, it is more like a playlist from an unintended journey of enlightenment with an added opportunity to discover a renewed zest and brilliance in your days, months, and years regardless of the order of things to come.

Welcome to *THISday*.

Playlist

"What day is it?" asked Pooh.

"It's today," squeaked Piglet.

"My favorite day," said Pooh.

—*A. A. Milne*

Contemplating THISday

Today is my favorite day, too. When done to its fullest, THISday can be so differ-ent from yesterday and nothing like what tomorrow will be. It is my favorite day because it is the only day I can do something about. THISday is also the logical and straightforward philosophy for an otherwise illogical and dastardly daily dilemma of regret, broken promises, wayward thoughts, and unfulfilling life experiences.

Like most wayward thoughts, streams of consciousness will abundantly flow always—and all ways—with words and meanings amok. I am no different. My words and ideas will hit these pages like prose in sequences, tangents, and eddies—not too dissimilar to your words and thoughts. But do those words and thoughts define us? Damn right, they do.

Do you speak, think, or express yourself like a Hemingway or a Fitzgerald? I don't. Do you believe yourself to be a Jane Austen, a Mark Twain, or a William Shakespeare? I don't. But I am an aggregate of all of them. And of all the songwriters and portrayers, too. I am the sum total of everything I have ever seen, heard, and believed. They have all influenced me, and they hit me in waves—peri-odically, randomly—making me write things like:

"Who am I? We are all a lot of things, aren't we? Am I a man, a father, or a son? I am poor. I am wealthy. I am a husband. A friend. I am old, and I am young. I am a memory for some and a future for others. I am a face in the crowd, or an old photo . . . lost. I am a writer, a thinker, a creator, a client, a peddler, a mentor, and an advisor. I am a cheerleader. I am a player. I am everything to some. And I am nothing to most. Could I be just a spirit guide having a temporal cosmic and physical experience? Of all that matters, who I am may matter not. For this all to become matter requires space, weightiness, understanding, listening, and words—shared and experienced—in the present, in the now, while there still is time left. This is THISday. So for now, I am THISday. I am just like you. I am reborn daily until my last. I am open, and I am vulnerable, because I am present. I choose THISday because it's where the right here and the right now can affect every action a human being is capable of, as there are no capable actions in THISyesterday or THIStomorrow. So, I have decided this now, that is Who I Am."

Rhetorically, yes, "I can go there" because I have been influenced by Twain, (both Mark and Shania). Springsteen and Shakespeare. Elvis (Costello and the other one). Along with my parents, teachers, and friends . . . it's endless, really. But while those words could define me, or should define me, I don't often use them to paint who I am. I often use other, conforming and closed-ended, words and phrases. Who am I? I'm a busy person. An executive. A media ad agency CEO, co-founder, and entrepreneur. I am a copywriter, too! I am a basic business-minded and creative-writing hack with an insanely busy schedule—probably a lot like you. At times, unfortunately, I speak, think, and express myself as such. Amok. Busy. I say what I believe. Then, other times, I don't say enough, and I fear that it is those words that may define me.

I am nothing that you think I am. Don't you dare judge me. Still, you will. Then again, what I would have you believe about me is only as good as the words I have offered up to you. What are the words that anyone or everyone have told you? Every book and bible. Every story ever told. And you believed them? And you judged them. WHY? Because we love stories and gossip. We want to see the blood, as long as it's not ours. We compare and contrast. We judge. We can see ourselves empathetic to the tale, or we see only the pathetic tale as we stare down our noses with impunity. But as I prepare to peel back layers of the tales I share, my only true gains are my freedoms from the oppressed notions I once held in secret mission to have you think different of me than I truly am. What you get is up to you . . . It's just a matter of choosing. Since my rebirth . . . which now comes THISday, and every day, I ask, pray, and want my words to be consistent with every word I ever have spoken, with just a touch of added weightiness as each day's words age. I find that brave and bold. And learned, and fortunate. And then again, I find that we are all prostitutes haggling over price, and knowing now that I have lost friends and seducers while trying not to sell my soul.

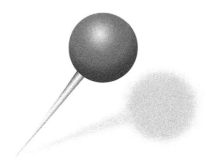

Hypocrisy and Ignorance are nearly impossible to self-diagnose.

Welcome to Machine

Is it fear or the fear of being defined—or, more specifically, inaccurately defined—that shall haunt us all? Whether that definition is self-assigned or passed to us by the judgments of others, it will be forever as present as our breath or our scent that is detected intermittently if not by us, by others.

It is a commonality of our entire species, through our experience of life, and to be alive and stay alive, that we must face fear. And not just fear for our mere survival, but outright and abject FEAR of judgment. For most of us, fear management is a daily, hourly, and even a moment-by-moment reality, whether you are conscious of it or not. Our thoughts, decisions, judgments, and mounted expectations can conjure full-fledged FEAR.

I am a marketer, and I work in the fear business. That machine built on the backs of countless souls who haplessly engineered the industrial complex of humankind. But then again, aren't we all cogs in the machine? As a marketer, much of my professional life is judged by what words, images, and meanings I can get into a thirty- or sixty-second message. I write and produce radio and TV commercials for a living. Making an advertisement can be a thankless task where the art and science of playing with and preying upon human behavior and societal commonality meet up with over-expectant corporate neediness while simultaneously asking people to buy into products and services that they didn't know they wanted when they woke this morning. Selling fear. *FOMO—the Fear Of Missing Out.* Fear of loss, unfulfilled needs, wants, and missed opportunity. What else did you think marketing was about?

So, assuming I can do all that successfully, I must now train others how to sell it through to you, the unsuspecting consumer. That's what I do. I do that over and over and over. I write, I produce. I coach. I train. I guide. I teach that not all fear is bad. Fear can be simplified and cognitively addressed. Re-scripted. Managed. It is called bravery.

"Our doubts are traitors, and make us lose the good we oft might win, by fearing to attempt," said William Shakespeare, the Bard of Avon, in the sixteenth century. In the twenty-first century, a radio/TV copywriter had to truncate that Shakespeare essence for the sake of time; so I wrote, "Fear Sucks!" It has hints of some modern panache, right? As I jest, I also give example of our loss. We have lost some sense of meaning with our language, and "our fears now grow like sun-drenched wildflowers in the fertile meadows of our souls." I mean . . . "Our Fears Are Running Rampant!" Is it that these modern and rampant fears have forced the hand of marketers to talk fast, sell hard, and change message so often? Is it because we have lost the ability to write engaging prose longer than thirty or sixty seconds, or that we have run out of words? No, it is merely that you have run out of listening.

Why Such a Story?

THISday is not just a story; they are my personal essays whose sum total provides some sense of what the "side of the record" of life can mean for you, today and now. You may recall that a *record* was a black plastic disk used to deliver music to our ears. In the radio business, the A-side of the record was the featured song, but the B-side, or the "flip side," was another song, often a completely different song picked to reveal the artist's breadth, or range. Some B-sides got heard and became hits for the artist, others flopped. B-Sides are out there to test the waters for the public to decide. For my stories you can choose any side as you wish, as long as you understand they need not be remembered, retold, or replayed, so long as they remind you of the A-side and B-side stories from your own life. If so, and in time, you will come to know the ways of being in THISday and so rely less on stories laden with near-certain fabrication, ceremoniously suspicious, subjective and requiring creative recollection, plot, and poignancy, as our stories almost always are lies by definition. Instead, our accounts told may one day become built from contexts of "what happened" and multiple-viewpoint facts, and not from what we make them mean. The lessons derived from others (as the lessons I've learned and share with you in this book) may shine on as an example of what is possible. Not as factual warnings of what might happen if you were to live the same story or experience, but as your own pure and true thought.

In THISday, honest words and shared thoughts teach us about our vulnerabilities, and how those vulnerabilities can powerfully create an openness and a possibility for sharing expanded thought and completion of those things we begin. In this pursuit, you will rejoice as we set free ourselves from the confines our "have-to" lists, chants, rituals, and affirmations and redefine our life's "must-haves." It is in this pursuit of the "unlearning of our conformity" we find the varied paths of enlightenment.

Playing the B-Side

If you can oblige me, please allow me to earnestly flip the record over, and I will sing you this soul-bearing song I think you should hear. You see, what I really want to know about me is this: I am the best marketer I know. I am the best marketer who, because of abject fear, hides behind the worst marketer I know. I am the worst marketer I know, because I don't market that I am the best. Or that I could be the best. From fear, I continuously stop myself. From fear, I have restrained efforts to step from behind the camera into the light. I have, by worded design, remained behind the scenes even when ample opportunities to make a move were presented to me. You see, I see myself differently because I think of myself differently because I speak of things differently. Before THISday, the words I used to communicate with others and to define me also forged my thoughts, and my feelings. Those thoughts and feelings forged my persona and being. And while thinking differently and speaking differently are really awesome traits for creative marketers, my doubts became my traitors and confined me into the shadows of a false security. Here, I became comfortable, and I became right by not having to talk about myself because it felt inauthentic, boastful and downright scary. Thinking differently and speaking differently to closed-minded people presents formidable risks for new connections, or new accounts. It poses risk to feeling understood. And it was there that I hid. It was there that I mitigated risk. It was there that I waited for sunlight, hoping to be found, and again, hoping it does not shine so bright as to expose me as a fraud who was neither the best nor the worst, but instead a person who settled with being average.

I want to say that. But no one speaks today with such openness. As I write these words and review them a thousand times, doing what every person should do with theirs, I am scared to death . . . and yet you are reading about my most sheltered thoughts. It is not heroic for me to do so, but it has required a journey of pursuit and tribulation to find the tiniest bit of bravery; and there it is, a part of my repertoire of most vulnerable secrets for everyone to hear. I am exposed. Every time I play my B-Side, my ego-driven fear dies just a little more; it is now my requirement to thrive.

Back to the A-Side

THISday, and in spite of the ever-present fears, I take on the marketing and influencing challenge passionately and with a curiosity to unpack its inner workings like a watchmaker would look to examine a clock that ran slow. To me, marketing is a snapshot personification of our humanness. It is communication, information, and education. It is a mystery to see what makes us tick and what makes us respond. Stimulus and Response. Correlation and Causation. That's science. To help figure out how to make that work for our customers and our people, well, that is where science and magic happen for me and for those I work with. I am proud that those words have defined much of my professional life and much of my personal life. But not all of it.

Through my personal and professional life, I have been privileged to have a few great coaches, teachers, and friends, and privileged to have a few terrible ones, too. Exposing the "goods" in our life is equally important as revealing the "bads" in our life. Are they not the A- and B-sides of the same record? Perhaps. But in life, when your record gets played, you can't be sure that both sides will be heard, or what will be remembered—if anything—by continuously asking, *"Does anything I say matter?"*

Of Magic, Music, and Marmalade

I can't perform magic, I can't play the guitar, and I can't make marmalade like my mom . . . and it drove me nuts. Those are just a few things throughout the years I have tried to learn; and over the years, I have too learned to quit. Today, while I pray to find more and more things to quit, I continue to be wild over the mystery of magic, and I hear music and song more deeply, and I savor so much of life's flavor.

In doing so, I have found more things to love as I let go of my wanting to be *like*. I didn't need to know the trick in order to love the magic. I didn't need to learn the chords to love the song. I did not need to know magic or song to speak of my love for it.

And while you read my words, I have no idea who you need me to be like. But I do not want to be like anyone anymore. I have tried. And I am quitting that, too.

What I am not quitting, I am not quitting to my pursuit of the words that help you find THISday. And again, I am no Twain. But I can tell stories, too, with my voice, and my words, for I can no more fear the attempt, and therefore, I shall quit no more.

Like my mom's marmalade, there isn't a "just follow-these-simple-instructions" to THISday. There is no elevator pitch. If your life's game says you need info downloaded fast, I must inform you that you are likely, and unknowingly, a pawn in yet a bigger game of manipulation. So know this, of which I am telling you, I am not selling you magic beans. THISday ain't a pitch. And if it were, you could not, and would not, catch it in a moment or two. THISday takes as much explanation as teaching someone the meaning of balance if they haven't before experienced balance. Explaining THISday is like trying to explain or prove love. Balance and love—you understand them, know them, feel them ONLY when you experience them. Maybe that is my elevator pitch: "It's like balance—you'll know it when you get it." Then again, maybe it skips off you like a stone across water. I am not dissing my own ideas or giving you an easy "out." What I am saying is, not all of us are open to receiving information at an equal pace, if ever. Same with balance and love. And similarly, the lessons of THISday are a grace to pursue and never catch. Like balance and love, THISday can change life's outcomes and experiences, and in time change you. Or not.

28

As much as I want to give THIS to you, and the world, I cannot make you receive it, for it is not mine to give. Just like I want things for my kids, there are things I can undoubtedly share but cannot be sure you or they will get. But still, I give. I will provide you with examples of how it sounds, yet the hearing and listening and understanding will be up to you. I will give you examples of what THISday looks like so you may see it, but it will be yours to seek. I will illustrate them in black-and-white, and you can add the color along your path to your THISday, as you will not experience what I have. However, you will no doubt glean absolute and measurable, perhaps even unexplainable differences in your personal effectiveness, your happiness, your outcomes, your output, and your outlook on everything.

And let's be real, we can make our mom's recipes like she did. We just need to quit quitting, or quit comparing our efforts to be "like." Enjoy the magic you make.

Wordsmithing the Editor

Could you imagine if Mark Twain or Pink Floyd wrote ad copy today? Although, while sixty-second ad copy wasn't a "thing" in Twain's day—he was widely heralded for penning some poignant one-liners back in the late 1800s, like saying that *common sense ain't so common*. But even Twain had his influencers. Perhaps it was Voltaire who similarly wrote the same line a century and a half earlier. Then in truth, the fact that common sense hasn't been, well, common has been common since AD 130, when the Roman poet Juvenal first wrote that there was *not a more uncommon thing in the world than common sense*. And I can only think that that was something Juvenal heard from his dad, over and over! And that's how words go, they linger and influence and inspire. And too, it makes me wonder if Mark Twain or David Gilmour wrote TV ads today, would we get their message? Would we understand their meanings? Or, would people even care?

With this concern, my discussions with my editors went like this: "If I write as I speak and like I think, which 'ain't so common,' and I write with varied intonation, slow and fast, with odd word arrangements that are not pleasing to literary rule makers, or rule followers, how do I deliver an original message that challenges conformity?"

Ugh! Book editors have so many rules. Many of these rules are the same rules that got smashed when Shakespeare and Twain showed up. More rules fell at the poet's pen, followed by the songwriters. Artists like Bob Dylan, Pink Floyd, The Doors, and Bruce Springsteen all produced game-changing contributions to the art of saying what needs to be told and how. Including what needed to be said, and when. Their words can last a lifetime, and then some. Their words can give you perspectives never before realized, and change you as they have me, and like they still do. Great songs and great artists and writers make me think, challenge my preconceived notions, and ask me to study my world and how I fit in. Springsteen, Dylan, Roger Waters and David Gilmour, Jim Morrison, Elvis Costello, Neil Peart, Sam Smith, Khalid, and countless others share their perspectives so vividly, and do so from their life experiences, observations, and struggles — and were influenced by those that preceded them. Somehow, each of them had the gumption to write something, say something, and do something new and different in a different style and a different way. Bob Dylan's words fascinated an entire generation of people, and launched societal changes and spoke truth to power. Springsteen gave a voice to the voiceless and shared the strife of the blue-collared man.

Jim Morrison, Elvis Costello, and Neil Peart lent us insight into worlds we didn't know existed until they gave of themselves, no matter how strange. "People Are Strange," "(What's So Funny 'bout) Peace, Love and Understanding," and "Freewill" are lyrical testament to this fact: Without these songs and words, the world would appear more like a room without a window — existing, but without a view of anything not formed by man.

And from these musical influences, we can witness and provide testament that the evergreen spirit of shared words flourish with new voices like Sam Smith's and Khalid's, who awaken us and replenish us with their words and give us a sense that so many more authentic words, stories, and songs must be said, shared, and sung without constraint because the absence of any one voice is tragic, and the conformity of any one voice is tragedy's muse.

These artists are authentic, vulnerable, and real. And if they had not spoken, written, or sang, then who would they be? Where would they be? Would they be fighting the critics, those traitors whose opinions matter to so few? And if they conceded to the conformists, would they be invisible, like those of us who stay in line and not speak up or out? Would they be like those of us who feel quashed or tamped down by those who appear to be on a rung above us, wielding some semblance of power over us? No, these artists took a path that most would rather skip; they bucked the norms, and each played, read, and sang their words to anybody who would listen. They performed in small crowds, in clubs, and on street corners. Why? Because what they needed to say mattered, even if it mattered only to them. In time, each would grow to entertain millions while at the same time influencing countless others in all aspects of society— and they would inspire at least one guy I know. That would be me; and fifty years later, *THISday* shows up on my editor's desk. Poetry, it is not. Different, it is. Influenced by all before who thought, said, and shared their voice for the first time with the world. *THISday* begins by understanding that we all have something say. We must find our words, and speak them. Or don't, and wallow in ignorance, misery, or even worse: unknown mediocrity.

Belong to the
Pursuit, and
Not to the Tribe
and enlightenment
will be yours to find.

The Clampdown

Regardless of our life's station, we are BUSY! That is what's common. Kids, jobs, travel, meetings, family demands, exercise, and spirituality. It is stressful. Making money, paying bills, forgetting what day it is, and at times just silently praying for the weekend or the pipe dream of a few minutes of quiet time—personal time . . . alone . . . with your phone . . . in the bathroom . . . safe. Maybe you have a fantasy of one day unplugging and living a dream life on the beach. All the while, your mind is still going a thousand miles an hour, processing your life's "musts" and dealing with your dramas!

Up until my early forties, at times, I thought my life to be grand. At other times, well, it felt like it was not. While some may think being a media CEO and ad writer would be a "glam-jam," fast-paced, and exciting-existence career path, I could equally say that BASE jumping for YouTube views would be just as compelling—though I wouldn't want to do it every day. Maybe both are better ideals to merely observe. At this point in my career, I've found reflective irony in much of my career path. I became responsible for the training and advancement of other people's lives via their career development, business development, corporate development. I molded people and corporations to behave in ways that I needed them to be, how they should be. I loved training and coaching.

THISday

But why was I doing this? I suppose early on in my life I could have claimed, "I was doing this because I knew no better." But my now-aged reflection sheds new light on the case. It wasn't because I didn't know better; I was merely behaving in the ways that I believed someone else needed me to be.

That's how early life goes. We model and mimic. We do as we are told, wait our turn, and make single file lines. We are formed to conform. Then later on, typically, they don't tell you what to do anymore. You should know better now. The formal educations are complete—another brick in the wall. Real life begins. The game is on. Compete.

Soon after, I discovered, or at least suspected, that in a way, there was some *go-along-to-get-along* coercion going on in this world. A solid sense that a scam was going down. A guttural realization that a still-unfolding game or trick was being played over and over on me. A rich and complex game that had been played so long, that I really hadn't noticed the "setup," or how some of us now relate to this "coercion" as being the "norm" in normal life. We proffered the fears as, "Don't be weak. Don't show emotion. Exude confidence. Drive a nice car. Wear designer clothes. Have straight hair. Be popular. Fake it until you make it. Don't do that; you will embarrass yourself."

We learned to parrot quotations and phrases, like "that's life," or "that's just the way it is," and so on. In many, many ways they are true sayings. In many, many other ways they're outdated conformity hooks and clichés that are lousy excuses for not living THISday to an elevated and life-fulfilling potential. Popular culture joined in and wrote songs and made advertisements to advantageously anesthetize us with an onslaught of propaganda full of mediocre and mind-numbing words to influence our thoughts and feelings. The corporations pined for your eight-to-five life while leveraging its growth and dependence upon investors, while governments minimized accountabilities and responsiveness to its constituents needs. Why? Because there was money to be made.

It was a clampdown, the racket, the game. Exactly like The Clash sang about. It was a win for the strong and abled few, once again built on the backs of those willingly influenced to buy in to the game. And while it is reasonable to argue the human, humane, and societal importance and benefits of this game; it was argued in the shadows of the game's dark underbelly—where you could sense many becoming overwhelmed by the sheer vastness of the scam that they would have at one time wanted to die to defend. And lastly, there are those who succumb to resignation, feeling that their human capital was chewed up and spit out. Feeling that there was no more growth, except for those willing to play the game harder, and more voraciously to an unknown end. To conceal these felt realities or consequences of the coin toss, or to listen to the person perceived to be a rung above us—because "that's just the way it is," was the glass ceiling of enlightenment. They became the whitewashed words that we now must shoulder, fitted somewhere between an "effort to avoid taking responsibility for things we don't want to deal with honestly and forthrightly—either for ourselves or others" and "revolt."

By playing the game, which we are conditioned to from birth, we prepare to compete and are put on a path of expectation set forth by others to gather experiences, education, behaviors, skills, and competencies to see where and at what level we can enter the game in the "real world." Then we live out our ordinary lives relating to this game as the game they call life. But, of course, as in any game, there is a score. A toll. Winners and losers. But haven't you noticed how it often doesn't turn out that the good guys win and the bad guys lose? And by the way, which is which, and who is who? This is spooky dystopia shit.

Put Me In Coach

How is the game going for you? How deep into the game are you? What is the objective of this game? And, that person, you know, the one perceived to be a rung above us, well, what if that person is inexperienced, incompetent, or just a plain idiot?

In my game, I have won some, and I have lost some. I have made some great plays. And other times dropped the ball. I was deep into the game, too. I was a strong advocate for the "this is the real world" system of life. So much so, I trained and taught others how to "say this, when they say that," and how to win, beat others, and get more from the game. Yet over time, many of us realize that we are being played, or that the rules keep changing.

We sense that the game is unfair at times, and we think, "Is this it?" or, "Is this the best I can do?" How do we get ahead of the game? Or at least get in control of the game? Can we change the game? Many of us see or sense what's going on. The spin. The cheating. The hypocrisy. We think—and we create ideas, thoughts, ways of being, and so forth—about a way out or a better way through. For some, we may even want out of the game but can't see how. I felt that way. I did.

Many times, I thought to overhaul my whole "life's approach" in order to augment or enhance how I can play this game of life. I tried several times. I still try. A quasi-reinvention here. A seminar there. Faith-based. Faith-less. A refocusing of what I thought

I knew, and what I could do, you know, to change my path. My game. I have tried counseling, and how-to books, drugs, alcohol, job changes, moves, religion, friend upgrades, and unfriending. But the game plays on, as it forever will.

Whatever game it is, we have a choice. We can watch it. Get out of it. Or play it better.

All You Have Is
Because Someone
Spoke Up.
All You Don't Have Is
Because Someone
Has Not.

We Can Work It Out

So the question remains: "How do we play *the game* better?" As we ripen and age, we undoubtedly gain perspective. Most perspectives are simply hidden from our sight and our thoughts, only revealed in time—our own time. Some of us don't ask for others' perspectives, but people want to hand them out to you, like a pamphlet or a meme you happen across. Even the elders hand us sage advice, but we seem immune to such talk from old people. Shame on them. What do they possibly know? One time, this really old man told me to "not take advice from someone more messed up than you." I laughed. Then one day, I realized my dad was right! He had perspective, while I was somewhat reluctantly gathering mine.

Yes, I play the game. I play to the very best of my informed senses, perspectives, and ability to create and share rules advantageous to all players. Pollyanna, I am not. No false sense of optimism or pitch for you to buy anything you may think I am selling. There is enlightenment, but it is not mine to proffer. If you are breathing, the game is on, and I coach to play the game, not to win it, for there is no winner if winning requires a loser.

¡Oye, Como Va!

Yes, I play to win, I am competitive. But the art of winning-for-all is the version I pursue. And I need to add a crucial caveat for understanding the core of my existence and foundation for building my relationships, my family, my business, my life. What you didn't know is that the lion's share of my expertise in words, meanings, listening, and in business, marketing and ad writing, is that it is almost entirely done in Spanish.

Oh, it gets better. While this may be moderately interesting, the really intriguing thing is that I don't speak Spanish. At least, not fluently. Yes, I'm gringo!

Now, I will dodge this fact with the all-too-common stories about how I "understand a lot," but, come on—I own a Spanish-language advertising agency. I write and direct Hispanic radio and TV personalities and superstars to do my commercials for my clients.

In 2007, I won the Medallas de Cortez, an award from *Radio Ink* magazine, as "Hispanic Radio's Sales Manager of the Year." The industry's highest acknowledgment for Hispanic radio marketing. And in 2017, two of my clients were listed in the top twenty radio advertisers in the US, according to Nielsen rankings. One of them in the Top Five.

These are proud accolades of my work, but approximately—no, absolutely zero percent of my work-life successes would have occurred without the careful and deliberate collaborations fostered by an inclusive "everyone wins here if we figure out how to work together" dialogue and way of communicating. Zero.

To win, and to create winning for self and others, is a matter of new and varied views, lenses, and perspectives. Without them, we know and understand less and less while our minds atrophy. It isn't until we embrace a pursuit of understanding that we are free to unlearn conformity. As we do, we may relearn that every story we were told is invalid, in error, or told with leveraged untruths. We may come to learn that nearly every thought, or thoughts that those stories produced are chided, and every word rendered fallacious until we rewrite and align the words, meanings, thoughts, and feelings into a powerful construct that benefits all, advances perspective and caring. Like the unlearning of Columbus's discovery of America, or the slave-trade stories of 1619 (rather, the lack thereof), each require deconstruction and re-scripting, to be told with balance and accuracy no matter what or how confronting the truths become, for it is the truth we shall forever pursue, not just a tale.

Time (it's 11:11 again)

It was 11:11 p.m., again, and as I lay awake, I thought about creating a new life for myself and for those who wanted to be in it. It was, after all, my world. At that time, when I was my former self, say in my teens and twenties, my world seemed untethered and I floated upon storybook outcomes until I transitioned to this "real" life. And as I arrived into "real" life, while I would no longer be corralled and herded, the systems of measurement and expectation would grew exponentially. In all my youth, while I stood in single file lines and waited for "turns," in real life, it seemed like a summer breeze, as I simply performed as asked, showed some initiative, and my time in line for "my turn," and "my promotion" just whizzed by. I seemed to have been programmed to be on fast-forward. And as I looked procedurally or chronologically at what was "due" in my life at this stage of the game, man, I was killing it! Apparently, I was good at real life.

But then, at thirty-five years of age, either I was alive but not living or I was living but not alive. I can't be quite sure which is most fitting of my former self.

I would like to say that at age thirty-five an aha moment fast-tracked and transformed me. It did not. I did not hear a voice or see premonitions or get a buzz in my belly. The only thing notable and alarming—and distracting—was my damn alarm clock! It seemed like every time I looked at it, the time was 11:11. No, my alarm clock wasn't only alarming me, it was pissing me off. And my watch, too. And the radio, and the game clock at the football stadium. And nearly every football game on TV. And the Southwest Airlines flight number between El Paso and Dallas. The address of my wife's new friend. The time stamp on my credit card receipts. Why was it always 11:11?

First, you get the words,
   - then you get the thoughts,
   - then you get the feelings,
   - the perspectives,
   - the mind-body-spirit,
   - the friends, the family,
   - the wealth, the health
   & the life.
THISday

The Lenses of THISday

It is amazing what we find when we seek with purpose. It is amazing when we miss the forest for the tree. Perspectives work just the same. Sometimes, we get fixated on seeing what we are looking for and we become oblivious to all that is around us. Maybe it's like a murder-mystery novel that has you almost sure whodunit, then, in a twist of circumstance, surprises you with a reveal that you could not have imagined. "How could I have missed it?" you wonder as you reel back through the story lines and clues missed or misinterpreted.

Perspective is the power of focus, and it's coachable. It's a skill set I discovered as a sales trainer and perfected as a single dad. All of our senses have a wide scope of capabilities, much like a zoom lens on a camera. With our eyes, we can see near and far as they adjust focus for subject clarity. With our sense of smell, we can detect scents both strong and faint. And we can taste and isolate very distinct flavors. We can feel a microscopic thorn as easily as a bad vibe. We can hear a vast range of sounds, from a distant train to the slight ringing in our ear. All senses can zoom in and out with our intent focus. Focus is an extremely important and innate human tool. Each of us has the varied ability to focus with a precision that allows us to complete tasks with expedience, efficiency, and accuracy. Our motor skills allow us to function in near-autopilot mode while we concentrate on more detailed thoughts or actions. Driving a car, shaving, typing, and jogging are just a few examples of our true multitasking skills at work while our thoughts are focused elsewhere. Our multitasking skills end there. "Go on, I am listening. I just need to text this message," is not multitasking. It's an all-too-common scene at any restaurant or coffee shop with groups of people sitting together, each on a mobile device, believing they are "multitasking." They are not, as each "just a moment" takes them away to a more focused task, and farther from being present for you. When we do come back, we try to fast-forward our absorption, expression, and/or interpretation of missed information, and we therefore may jump to conclusions. Our perspective is playing "catch-up." We quit seeking, stop listening, or start speaking before we know what there is to know. We do this every day. Sometimes, we guess right. Most times, it's a forgiven "swing-and-a-miss." Too many times, we miss the grandeur of the forest.

46

A camera lens can always find its focus, once it finds its focal point. Then, with just little effort and adjustment, that lens can capture clear and brilliantly defined images, memories, and stories. From that same position, that camera with a different lens can find new focal points to consider and capture and see and understand more as well as differently.

We have the same capability to see things from multiple perspectives. Sometimes. But we are also taught to focus—quickly. Sometimes, we do that, too.

The power of focus I learned most definitively as a single parent while trying to herd stammering and yammering kids going this way and that. It's a special "task game" that was named "Hidden Mickeys." I also used the task game in sales training under a less childish name, of course, but it used the exact same mechanisms. It works very simply like this: Make a specific request of others to find something so specific that it detracts from all other distractions. In the case of the "Hidden Mickeys," kids would search for rocks, stones, and pebbles that resembled the Mickey Mouse ears. I made it fun and the reward was twofold: The kids stayed busy and quiet! Brilliant. Until the kids wised up and started asking for bigger payouts. But for a while, man, were they focused. Real child-guided lasers, searching millions and millions of stones, rocks, and pebbles for Mickey Mouse. The sales reps I trained weren't as cute as my kids, but the outcome was the same: It got them to focus on tasks important to my "real" life goals, which was finding me money.

Me, at a sales meeting: "$100 for the person who logs the most new business calls today."

The sales reps: Money-finding-guided lasers staying busy and quiet! Brilliant.

There is a time for focus.

Then there is a time for perspective.

47

The Power of Perspective, Episode 1

Like the mystery novel, perspective can move us in many magical ways. And its essence is our truest beauty to behold—when we remember to use it. In 1972, the Apollo 17 astronauts captured the first-ever photograph of Earth, in a photo shot of a lifetime titled *The Blue Marble*. This one photo changed the entire perspective of man's understanding of our world by having us all look at our planet from a vantage point so far from home and distances previously unfamiliar. The photo was shot from a spaceship orbiting the moon, and it showed our planet as it magically floated in the darkness of space against a background of stars and distant galaxies, giving us the first-ever sense of our little rock in space: our home. You've seen it. It's probably your screensaver now.

That one perspective changed us. It was a new lens that conjured infinite questions of our existence and our place in the universe, both literally and spiritually. For some, this new look evoked fear and a certain loneliness or sense of isolation. To others, it inspired bigger dreams and a more challenging pursuit of questions unanswered. Today, *The Blue Marble* is a reminder of newly gained perspectives when striving for greater understandings. Then again, this perspective is just a milestone of discovery—no more revealing or impressive as is learning about Isaac Newton's discovery of gravity.

Closer to home, an ophthalmologist near you uses a device nearly every day called a "Phoroptor" that refracts light (through a lens, duh . . .) and allows the doctor to try on different lenses to determine the correct ones your eyes require to see clearly. The doctor quickly and efficiently clicks, flicks, and positions a near-infinite array of lens coordinates to get your eyes to see perfectly. The advent of the Phoroptor in 1920 forever changed humankind and our ability to see with clear vision throughout our life-time. That is a big deal, even though we feel it is no big deal anymore.

But knowing perspective and having perspective are way different animals. So, too, is "giving" perspective and "offering" perspective. It seems, sometimes, our perspectives get stuck and we lose sight of what we have, and what we can gain with new perspective.

Indeed, perspective and all of its boundless discoveries and provision we enjoy is a genius gift bequeathed to us. By our good fortune, we were born, and borne to it. But times have gotten short, and fast and efficient—and expedience tells us to find Hidden Mickeys and not Blue Marbles.

49

Of Knowing

Knowing is a lens we all have. We all see through a knowing lens every day. We know red means stop and green means go. We know not to put our hand on a hot stove. Knowing is experiential. We know a lot. We know what we know, and we even know what we don't know. But none of us doesn't know what we don't know, right? So let's use our "knowing" lens and pursue what we know. We know about our world, our environment, and let's say, our neighbor. Good.

Now, what do you know about your partner? Your needs. Your wants. People. The game. Your strengths, thoughts, worries, ideals, job, passions, gratitude, commitment, ego. What do you know about yourself, your enemy? How about your rights? Your wrongs. Your hypocrisy. What do you know? And knowing you, I bet you have already started to answer. We love knowing. We dislike not knowing. But you know that, right? Knowing and the want for knowing is a never-ending rabbit hole to explore as we all want to "know what we know." But knowing is just one perspective.

I Now Know . . .

I now know that perspective is perpetual, yet experiential and therefore temporary, or momentary. I know now, it takes conscientious work to keep perspective in perspective. It is both personal and not personal. And I now know that not all people who see, seek. Not all people who hear, listen. Where you are in the game is a subjective perspective. What you see and feel has changed, is changing, and will continue to change. However, unchecked, those who don't seek, get blindsided. Those who have not heard, lose their path. And what is heard? It is the inherent "noise" of the game — the constant drumbeat from the molding of our youth — that prepares us to play the game. The sirens, whistles, and authoritative voices from the sidelines when we start playing the game. Then there is this voice in our heads that sometimes won't shut up. It can be deafening. Maddening and life-limiting.

I say blessed are those who can grasp perspective early in life. I didn't. Blessed are those who grasp it anytime in life. I think I have. Perspective and THISday doesn't come with age; though it does take years to acquire, if at all. Perspective takes practice, guts, and tutelage. It takes a risk, without which you will get the same old days and the same old stories. The same old love. The all-too-common unremarkable, mediocre life. Getting to THISday is not easy. It's a process that seemingly comes in waves. It is a "process" with virtually NO RULES; just ideas, examples, and reminders.

THISday

I cannot teach you vulnerability or honesty, but I can show you what it looks like. Beware, it can be scary as f*ck. It can also be your key to ultimate freedom and pathway to a place called "enlightenment."

The "enlightenment," as I call it, I can only describe in stories. My stories. But like all good stories, they have an ability to open something up in others. It could simply be like group therapy without the group. So I share THISday because I am fixing me. I believe that that's a worthy enough cause. I do this not to fix you. That is your job. And that is a worthy job, too. I do know you will get something from the stories. What that is, is yours to share in your world. I can only share what I can share, then most humbly cheer for you. It is your life. Your game. Your song to write and your song to sing.

THISday, I contend, that for changed behaviors, different outcomes, a changed future, and a change in the game, we must try new things at times. Trying new things can be hard. You have tried self-help seminars and juicing. A grand *detox* . . . of your wallet. Most of us want a multistep process, a list of "have-tos" or "musts" or some other shortcut, affirmation game full of hope for some instant gratification. THISday, we are having a different conversation about a different cheer we should know, and by doing so, we will add a new twist to the old game for a chance at a new and better outcome. A new listening that searches for a new understanding. A new chance for a new life.

It's a Deathtrap

In 2002, my new life was in an old city. My wife and I were completing a tumultuous tour of four US time zones. In 1995, she and I did not know we were chartered for a seven-year escapade launched immediately upon our return from our honeymoon. That same year, my first management job succumbed to corporate raiders and prompted me to seek a new gig. For this job, I searched far and wide and selected the best fit for me and my new wife in Portland, Oregon . . . 1,700 miles from home. The offer came fast, and the money was low, but it was anywhere other than El Paso, and that was the point. I was set to prove I was good at this game. That, and it was the only offer I would receive; but too late . . . I took the gig. So what, I didn't need to be in management any longer . . . just a regular ol' sales job was enough to make me feel like I belonged. What a move. What a change of life. What an opportunity. An opportunity to conform, in another town. This was truly *real life* for tramps like us. You know, a new city. A new wife. A new start.

Even though we were newlyweds, we decided it best for me to find a place and start work while she busily took to selling our El Paso home. In fact, my new wife didn't even visit Portland before I made the job commitment. As it turned out, the home sold faster than expected, and she was able to join me in Portland just thirty days later, along with the news that she was expecting. That, too, was also faster than expected!

THISlove

On the day Hannah, my first child, was born, my mother was with my wife and me in the delivery room. My daughter was born, swaddled, and handed to me for the first time. In my arms was a new possibility, a new life to color the world. Infinite emotion rushed in. Unknown feelings in a crashing wave of warmth. Just two minutes before her birth, I didn't have those feelings. Now I did. I just learned the secret of what most every dad knows. The secret that every dad throughout history has known but which couldn't be shared until you experienced it firsthand. I was now a dad. And now, in a split second, I knew. And it spilled over me. It poured into me. I had to have been glowing.

It could not have been any better. That is, until my gentle mother, she with her teary eyes and calm, slow, and restrained voice of pure sweetness, said, "Now you know . . ." She paused while holding back her tears. "And now you know how much we love you."

Ka-Pow! Brain explosion! I should melt any moment now.

In my life, and my good fortune, I have loved, and I have known love. But now a wave of new information about love, of all things, came crashing into existence, suddenly, unexpectedly, and magically. The listening and understanding and displacing all that I knew of love. I got it! I felt it. I got a gift, and I experienced THISlove for the first time.

Clear and honest words said, heard, felt, and received at a time when they could only make sense of what the love of a child was really like. And to know that my mother carried those feelings for my lifetime and to then gift me with the understanding of what a parent's love was about, well, it changed me. Something cracked open in my soul. The light came in and illuminated unknown spaces in my present moment. So much so that I would long to stay in that present moment forever.

Although, like how all great moments turn to great memories, I would now know THISlove forever. Like learning balance when you ride your first bicycle, the feeling and understanding lasts forever.

But all of this was just that, a memory. I haven't ridden a bike in years.

Parenting

Many years have passed since those not-to-be-forgotten days. My daughter and son are now grown and have left home. But the love, caring, and neediness of raising children has never once subsided from that very first day.

Back then, I insisted, as I still do today, I wasn't raising a girl; I was raising a woman, and I wasn't raising a boy; I was raising a man.

That they are now gone from the home doesn't mean I am done honoring that commitment, far from it. I hope I am never done.

Raising a son to a man, and a daughter to a woman is tough. Doing this is as frustrating as telling a kid to clean their room for the millionth time. With each time believing that maybe this time it will stick and that it will never have to be mentioned again. But a million times reminding your kid to do something, anything, takes time. It adds up. It takes its toll. Oh, and I have paid. Haven't we all?

"Will they ever learn?" Because I can nag, and I can yell. I can fake cry, I can real cry, and I can guilt them into submission. I have a commitment, and I CANNOT give up or submit to letting them NOT clean their room! Or to become a man, for that matter. Or a woman. Or whatever. Will I?

Maybe I am trying too hard. Or I am too hard-core about this. I mean, maybe. Ultimately unnecessary? Probably.

Look, is the "whatever" nag you are stuck on going to change their behavior? Teach 'em real good? Is it going to matter or improve their life? Change the world?

Maybe. Maybe not.

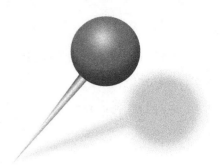

Meaning is to Understanding what Wanting is to Having

So what is on the other side of this "whatever" nag?

Good question. Was it my commitment to manhood for my son? Or was it for my daughter to finally become a woman? Was it for independence? Was it for their own good? I mean, really, aside from being their dad, do I really get to say when that magic moment happens? Do I get to decide when they graduate to Manhood or Woman-hood? Hell no.

    Why is it that as kids, we live our youth unabridged and full of self-expression, then at some unknown yet definitive point, we transfer our outward selves to an inward cell full of our known limitations? Tell me, is it an act or a conversation that closes the door on possibility and ends our youth? Why, as parents, do we think we can avoid re-creating for our kids the same traps our parents made for us? Traps about money or cleaning your room. Traps about what men are supposed to do, and about what ladies are supposed to do. Traps about what we can and cannot talk about. Why all the traps when we have so many options to speak, think, and feel differently from what was given to us in our formative years?

    I am committed to these kids for my whole life. That is MY love. That is a love that my children know, but not fully understand, though in time, will. That is the THISlove my mom bequeathed to me when my daughter was born. THIS is the love I pray I can give them. Now that I know, now that I understand THIS love, whence before I had only known a meaning of love. From this experience, I now get that MEANING is to UNDERSTANDING as what WANTING is to HAVING.

Like all things known and understood, once you know love, you cannot not know it. And most specifically with love, if you now know THISlove and you don't share it, then you are complicit in what you get. In this case, your adult child faltering in the face of challenges. That's on you! That's the whole committed-for-life thing. Yeah, that's on you.

Yet, when dealing with, say, young adult children, what can you do? Aren't you mostly powerless? Isn't the genie out of the bottle? You can no longer ground them or take away a privilege. That bus left the station. What power remains? What will you do and say to help them, guide them in the face of their challenges? Will you control them? Acquiesce to them? Will you still try to play the game for them?

When do you begin to share THISlove? At what age? What child? And not just for your children. What partner? What co-worker, stranger, or human? To whom and when do we dole out what we can give?

I profess you can stand with any child, at any age, and talk with them. You can stand and give "THISlove" to anyone, anytime. You have this superpower now. You can give love, support, and empathy. Kind and inspirational words. And that is all. There is nothing more. It is the most you and anyone can do or give. You cannot love for them, give for them, or do for them. You cannot play the game for them. You effectually are a cheerleader, and nothing more. You can cheer them on, indeed, but only from the sideline. Yes, this is the new you. Your forever roll as a cheerleader. Their cheerleader.

Give me a C-H-E-E-R?

Who is your cheerleader?

Who is your worst critic?

The answers to these questions matter. Getting to the real honest answer is vital. Yet, here lies one of life's great contradictions. The likelihood that you, or we, will ever "own" the honest answer is unlikely. Aside from its cliché-esque ask, it is arguably a moving target—a situational enigma and an answer that truthfully doesn't need to be solved. However, the questions are just important merely to be pondered, presented, and thusly exposed. Now the pursuit becomes a key focal feature of being "THISday."

The answer to question #1 should be YOU.

The answer to question #2 is also YOU, but it is that other voice in your head that sounds like you but is definitely NOT YOU.

If you answered correctly—awesome.

If you answered differently, I have just a few more words about cheerleading.

We Are Consummate Cheerleaders

We all are cheerleaders. And not just to our kids. We cheer for friends and bosses, for politicians and strangers. We support, vote for, give advice to, love, empathize with, and shout for others. That is what we are: cheerleaders for all those we care about.

Outside of ourselves (we are utterly awful at cheering for ourselves), we are "BE AGGRESSIVE! B-E AGGRESSIVE!" with our cheering. We are "PUSH 'EM BACK, PUSH 'EM BACK, WAAAAY BACK!" with those we cheer against.

But after years of doing the same cheers to what we cheer for and against, the cheers from the sidelines and the stands have lost their effectiveness. While we cheer for those who are playing the game, in the arena, on the field, we must remain affirmed that cheering is needed and is essential. But as we know, cheering for the sake of cheering doesn't necessarily give us the outcome we hope for, now does it?

Cheering on a football team is a sport. Cheering on a child is not. BE AGGRESSIVE, B-E AGGRESSIVE doesn't necessarily tell your team that their left tackle is getting his ass kicked by the other team's defensive end. And that he's taking a false step every time the ball is snapped and losing a fraction of a second while trying to get into position to block this guy's bull rush to the quarterback, now does it? If you could cheer like that, it might be helpful or more useful, but, more likely, that cheer would just sound weird. It wouldn't be as happy and fun sounding as the B-E AGGRESSIVE noise.

Yet we cheerleaders keep cheering, with fruitless outcome. In parenting, and in otherwise non-sporting situations, also known as "real life," our cheerLEADING must change. Our cheers must change. Constantly. Otherwise, the cheer will risk becoming more "ambient noise."

Our kids, our families, our bosses, our politicians, and all the things we care for require new cheerleading.

Are You Ready for THIS?

A key feature of understanding THISday is that it takes time and practice. THISday takes guts and calculation. THISday looks to create a new cheer, with different words, assembled in new ways. Like any type of cheering, we seldom get the outcome we hope for. But when the GAME is REAL (and it is), we should use real cheers that have a real chance to work. We should have real conversations, in real circumstances, for the chance of real change. A chance. Remember, as a cheerleader, you are on the sideline of someone else's game. Shouldn't we break through the noise? Yes! Not by being louder, but by giving our honesty, our empathy, our vulnerability, and our love.

Love Letter to My Son

All good stories told begin with the end in mind. This story, it has a beginning, which I purposefully skip because it is a twenty-year-long story you can perhaps accept has somewhat normal, trying, and, well, boring-ass details. And this story has no end. It is still unfolding. But you can readily assume this is a never-ending story of "THISlove" . . . the love I hold for my now-adult child, and therefore you will understand how I may have felt when our "normal" text conversation shifted unexpectedly from "What's up?," "How's school?," and "I need money" to one of doom and gloom.

Me: "U good?"
Greyson: "no, not really"
Me: "what's up"
Greyson: "nothing"

Then I get a text that was unusually long for any modern-day millennial; it was an exchange that illustrated how my son was feeling overcome with pressure, depression, and hopelessness over his college classes, his finances, his stress levels, and what I had so brilliantly determined as a result of the mismanagement of his time.

Then I text: "so what are you going to do to fix it?"

THISday

That wasn't a good cheer. Subsequently, that text was followed by—nothing. Not a word.

(30 minutes later)
Me: ?
Nothing. It was late, and I fell asleep.

The following day, I text again. Nothing. Another text. Nothing. A "WTF?" text. Nothing. The next day. Nothing. The third day. Nothing. I text his mother, "Have you heard from Greyson?" "No. He doesn't text me back," she replies.

Proof-of-life contact came after a week or so of silence, during which he had not answered any of my texts or calls. Any college parent may understand the escalation of concern inside me. With each passing day of ignored communication attempts, my blood pressure rose. I was pissed. Then *ding!* I woke to see who the hell was texting at one o'clock in the morning. I saw it was my son—and I jumped to respond.

You see, first, I was just glad he was alive. Truly. As I said my little "thank you, Jesus," the layers of backstory came bubbling up in an instant: I want him to get a job. I want him to get good grades. I want him to be happy. I want him to have fun at school. I want him to freakin' call me back! I have a lot of wants for HIM . . . really for ME. But, for him. I am cheering for him. Because I love him. But if I am being real—and I am being real—if he succeeds, I will feel better about me and my screwups in life. Because my cheer, well, it's about me—but for him, and really for me. Get that? Come on, stay with me here. It's 1:00 a.m., and my son just finally responded to me.

Greyson: "Hey, what's up?"

Now I will have a teaching moment. I *do* know what's best. I mean, what parent doesn't? But then again, I also know that the lie-laden tales of "how-to" parenting, aka overparenting or finger wagging, are bullshit and lead to parent-child division.

Me: "U good?"

So, with all my wants for my kid, and all my "know-best" bullshit, I could have responded in numerous ways. I chose "u good?"

I could have yelled. I could have griped, guilted, bemoaned, threatened, and added more pressure and stress. I could have sent money, or I could have moved him back home to the nest. I could have blown it off until the next day, or next week. Or I could have solved ALL of his "now, at 1:00 a.m." problems and made them go away . . . until the next problem came. Then repeat. Over and over again . . . until I die. I had so many options. But I texted like nothing had happened in the last week. Greyson offered no more drama. And I chose not to create any.

Me: "glad you're good, let's talk tomorrow. Love u"
Greyson: "K. Love u too"

After the text exchange, and the relief from knowing my kid was "good" after a week of parental "lockout," there was no way in hell I was going to sleep. I was still pissed. And I had tons to say. So I tore out of bed, went to my office, sat down, and composed my thoughts. Two hours later I chose a THISlove note, in an email, preceded by a text that said, "Check your email. xo" and I wrote:

My Dear Son,

A lot of things came up in my head tonight after texting with you.

Many things. So I thought to write a note to you about a few of those things.

Look, you will figure things out. Ultimately, you and only you will. No one will figure your shit out for you. I had to. I still do. What's in your head, you choose to have there. You can also choose to not have it there. I earnestly believe in you, even though you may not right now. I know you may question how it all will work out for you with school, money, stress, and all that other B.S. I believe in you for many reasons. Great reasons. And I have no doubt that tons of other people do too. You are not lacking love and admiration.

You are just in the shit right now. Things are flying at you faster and faster. School, demands for friends, work, money, studies, have-tos, and all that. So, get used to it. It's going to last awhile. Like, forever.

Money won't make it go away, so don't lament being poor for now. It's a good thing. You'll see. Somebody once said it like this: "Rock bottom will teach you lessons that mountaintops never will." I pray you get that. And I hope you remember that when you get to the top. Remember this too: Cheerleaders don't cheer for you; they cheer for themselves.

What I now and will forever believe by saying this is, "Of course I cheer for you! But I cheer for you, for me, because I think it may actually help you!" And I want to help you. Always. But I can't. I can't play for you. I can't study for you or work for you.

I can't take away your tears, your sadness, your pain, your fears, your woes, your worries, your bad thoughts, or your nightmares. Boy, I would if I could. But man, if I did—well, then you would stay a boy.

Comparisons don't do much good, either. Like when I say, "When I was in college, my mom only sent me $5 a month." None of those stories make you feel much better now. They don't help, I know. But it's still, oddly, me being a cheerleader. I say it, because I think it will help you. I now realize it does not. So here's the cheat sheet, as far as I can tell, and maybe this will help somehow:

Give yourself a break from "thinking" about this stuff.

Just Be. Then Just Do. If you can Just Be and Just Do, you will have IT.

I know I am going a little deep here, but, "Be" is the root of many words like: BEing, BEcause, BElong, and BEfore. Got it? "Be" is a point of singularity. "BE is the present, also, as in the presence. The place that you need to be BEfore the action, BEfore anything can begin, YOU are the point of singularity. Are you still with me?

It's also like peace of mind. Like mental calmness. Focus. Clarity. Inner Zen.

Then there is the "DO." DO is the action, without reason. DO is not a decision. It's the DOing of that thing that needs DOing. It is what Nike was getting at when they said, "Just DO it!"

Nike didn't say, "Make me do it!" or "Find someone to do it for you." No, I am pretty sure it was, "YOU FUCKING DO IT. YOU WANT IT? YOU FUCKING DO IT! You DO you. Nobody is going to do all this stuff you want for you!"

So putting it all together now, there then becomes the BE-DO-HAVE thing.

(Quick mansplaining here . . .) It's like when you work out, you know, you zone out. What is happening is that you BEcome quiet in your mind. You quit talking, and

you quit talking inside your head. The noise and chatter go away. Even if you have music playing in your headphones. You zone out. You calm down. You focus. You quiet down the lying voices and noise in your head. Then you DO. You work out. You BEcome calm and you DO exercises. You quit messing around. You think less and DO something. If you DO this well, over and over, day after day, everything starts to change. Little by little, everything changes. Yes, it hurts, and you are sore, and you want to quit sometimes. And you could—truly, you could. But you don't. You continue and then, the BE and the DO start producing the HAVE.

And look what you HAVE now! "Holy shit," is what I said today when you sent me that pic of you after your workout. Look what you HAVE done. Look how you HAVE changed. Look what you HAVE BEcome. You did it. You did the BE-DO-HAVE.

It works with tons of life's challenges, big and small.

70

Now quit fucking around and go BE who you want to BE.
BE a student. And if you want, BE a good one.
BE a good worker.
BE a good friend.
BE a good son.
BE proactive.
BE committed.
BE awake.
BE fun, funny, loving, grateful, giving, and graceful.
BE rich.
BE that guy.

CHOOSE to BE whatever.
Then DO that DOing that needs DOing.

Soon, you will realize you HAVE had IT always. Look, it takes a long time. It's frustrating. And it doesn't always work out like a fairy tale. But it might. And that beats the hell out of just talking made-up nonsense to yourself and putting energy-sucking thoughts in your head. Because what's in your head, you choose to have there. You can also choose to not have it there.

So choose the good stuff.

Choose the BE-DO-HAVE. Choose it every day. Choose it THIS day.

Love,

Your Cheerleader!

#ThatsMyBoy

Pretty cool letter, huh? "Proud dad" moment—no doubt, right? No. Not so fast. This was a choice and it was a risk at the same time. This was one of my kids!

This was about something way bigger than me. And, yes, it was about me, too. It was about choosing how I show up—what I say and do and how I cheer. This was about what I put in and what I could get in return, if I got anything at all.

Who would you be if you weren't being the person someone else wanted you to be? How does that cheer go?

It's a matter of perspective, right? But who controls the perspective and all its varied shades? You do! So I crafted a written conversation that was full of risk because it was different from typical conversations that ran through my head. If I was feeling anything, it was that I was pissed. He ignored me, and it scared the hell out of me! Does he know how I cried the day he was born? Does he know what I do for him, and what I have done for him? Does he know my sacrifice? Did he know what my mom had told me? That kid should have felt my freaking wrath!

What should I have said? How should I have said it? In what tone, with what words, how often or even at all . . . I had a choice. Millions of them.

You are your word,
and you are where
you are because
of the WORDS
you use, and
choose to believe.

I've Been Everywhere, Man!

As a Division I athlete, I *had* been everywhere. Arizona, Alabama, Oklahoma, Arkansas, California, Hawaii, and Australia, with the hustle and bustle of college football, a great group of guys, coaches, and life experiences that last forever.

But all of this was just that, a memory. Was I now heading nowhere, at an ever-increasing speed, destined to look back on the greatest days of my charmed life in a rearview mirror? Hell no! "Real" life was just ahead.

We left Portland on the next hopeful train headed east. Next stop Evansville, Indiana, with more news on the way. My son Greyson was born soon after we arrived, and THISlove reappeared and rekindled us for a time with the notions of normalcy. A new home, new friends, and a new opportunity to spin for fortune.

The corporate crusade was now noted as normal, too. It seemed that riding the waves of corporate consolidation was for the nimble hotshots, and I so wanted to be that guy. I bought into the game, telling, selling, and smelling for that next wave of prosperity to ride. This time, I was ready. My experience had me prepared. The next wave came soon and would shove me to Toledo, Ohio, then on to Richmond, Virginia, before the undertow would suck me back to El Paso once again.

Seven years have gone, like that—back to square one. And now the 11:11 is haunting me. Is it my doom?

The Power of Perspective, Episode 2

We all also see through an understanding lens every day. We understand red means stop and green means go, in addition to knowing it. We know there is a language called GERMAN, and we know we don't understand it, got it? So let's pursue some of what we understand. What do we understand about our world, our environment, our neighbor? Easy, right? What do you understand about your partner? Your needs. Your wants. People. The game. Your strengths, thoughts, worries, ideals, job, passions, gratitude, commitment, ego? What about yourself, your enemy? How about your rights? Your wrongs. Do you understand and see your hypocrisy? What do you understand? And knowing you, I bet you have already started to answer. We love understanding. We dislike not understanding. But you understand that, right?

Focus now. Hidden Mickey up ahead! It's time to change the lens.

Of Respect

Same game, new lens. Respect is also a lens that we all have. We all see through a respect lens from time to time. We respect that red means stop and green means go. We respect that there is a language called GERMAN, and we know we don't understand it. So let's find what we respect. What do we respect about our world, our environment, our neighbor? What do you respect about your partner? Your needs. Your wants. People. What do you respect about the game? Do you "Love the game, hate the player?" Do you respect your strengths, thoughts, worries, ideals, job, passions, gratitude, commitment, ego? What about yourself, your enemy, your boss? How about your rights? Your wrongs. What do you respect? And knowing you, I bet you have already started to respect the fact you haven't thought of things like this before. That's the lens called DISCOVERY, my friend!

Of Discovery

Discovery can be exhilarating and confronting. Perspective lens changes can cause seismic shifts in thought and create aha-making machines. And perspective shifts can build barriers. They seemingly occur naturally in our species as our human curiosities and wonderment invite us to question our existence, our experience, and our worlds. Who among us doesn't love to discover something new? Well, if it sounds so intriguing, why do we ever stop? This lens has launched discovery expeditions and fact-finding missions, as well as launching many missiles, arrows, and stones. Perspective changes have forged nations, social movements, and productive benefits for humankind.

I can always seek argument,
critique and wrongness.
Or, I can always find what
is good, right and kind.
For it is the hypocrite
who knows no shame
from judgement.

Of Heaven and Hell

There is a simple proposition of Christianity. It is that of a heaven and a hell: a place where the good people go, and a place for the bad people.

That simple proposition is anything but simple. In fact, it is a trap.

How perfect and convenient of a setup could there be for an eternal judgment of oneself AND of others. What a grandiose predicament for the haves and the have-nots—the good and the bad, the right and the wrong . . . And, of course, the judgment. There is the worry and the want, the fat and the thin, and then more judgment.

Us and them, left and right, stress and freedom, politics and religion, AND JUDGMENT! It can be quite all-consuming, as well as a hypocritical cesspool.

So, before you go get your pitchforks, allow me to remind you that our world is about CHOICE and free will. And it should NOT be thought of as a world predicated on judgment and division. And THISday, like this very day, should not be subjected to and sentenced by our histories and experiences. That is YESTERDAY . . . of which we cannot change.

Heaven and hell should not be a tomorrow thought, either—or a futuristic place you get to go someday in the future as determined by all the days in your past.

As we aspire to awareness and awaken in THISday, with your free will you can choose to be in heaven or in hell right now. Heaven and hell is a NOW place. It is here in real time, and you can have it now, in real time, if you choose it.

We are *not* in a state of suspension between two places. And we are not on trial awaiting judgment, fearful and worrisome of the final verdict. *No*, that is a conformity trap.

You are free, and you are not constrained . . . if you choose it. You certainly have heard people say, and tell uplifting stories about, how they have been to HELL and back—but we almost never hear people say they have been to heaven and back. Otherwise, they would have stayed, right?

Because there is no middle point between heaven and hell. There is no, I AM HERE in the middle, heaven is up and hell is down. It's binary. It's a superposition, in both life and death—and especially THISday. If it is your conformed belief that heaven is a someday place that you hope to go when you die, you may be missing out on some of the best of what heaven has to offer . . . right here and right now.

And it's so easy to choose. You can choose joy, exuberance and contentment, kindness, compassion, and caring—the embodiment of what I believe heaven to be— because you can create and manifest your heaven now.

You have had THIS. A taste of heaven. You know it; you have seen it. It's beauty, and it's warmth and love. It's abundance and it's healing. It's goodness. It's cleansing. You have also had a taste of the hell on earth. The fear, the evil, the hurtfulness and deceit. The senseless hate, jealousy, the killing, pain, and suffering.

Choose heaven now, or don't—it's still a choice, right? Or you can continue a lifetime of indictments of those stories we believe are true but are not and keep judging and denying as we make unwelcome; build fences; stop learning; dim the lights and smiles, the laughs; discount, manipulate; forget; and disconnect.

But know, choosing what to believe or follow or pursue does NOT make the other disappear. It is merely a shift in perspective that can lessen our judgments of others, and free us from the fantastic and fanatical stories that conform and trap and conceal our true potential, here and now . . . and it illuminates new paths to follow that are inclusive for all of us . . . not just some of us . . . and we can have either heaven or hell now.

Look, your NEXT life is as unknown as your LAST life was. Meanwhile, what in the HELL are you doing with THIS life, now . . . THIS day?! You are HERE, YOU ARE NOW . . . YOU ARE THISday! The place that yesterday envies and tomorrow longs for . . . Choose it. Choose to fill it with all of the heavenly goods you can conjure. Whatever your belief, you can believe in THISday: the place where you can give, think, thank, welcome, learn, play, laugh, sing, love, seek and share, honor, respect, and connect.

That sounds like heaven to me.

Breakdown, It's All Right

Those eleven years from twenty-four to thirty-five had melded together. Glimpses and imageries of who I was back then are remote, sketchy like an old black-and-white photo full of faces of people whose names you can't quite remember. Some faces you can't forget, and the highlights, of course, are in color, but even after so many moves, the kids, and the business of all my "conformity" . . . MAN, I just recall . . . everything was going exactly to the life plan! So I was told.

My wife apparently thought different.

11:11 was everywhere in my life . . . seemingly stalking me. Then it scared me. I canceled flight 1111 many times and took a less spooky flight, and I tore up those damn credit cards!

I was certain it had to mean something . . . but was it good? And why? And why, again, did I think it was weird that our friend couple's address was 1111?

Fuck, it hurt to discover 1111 was not a good sign in this case. Hell, I'd guess every divorce collects its toll. It cost kids. It cost friends. It cost money. And it would cost me my former life.

11:11 was more than a sign, it was a curse! How could it not be? "Fuck you, 11:11!"

The Way Back

While weighing life's options, I fell back on a few lessons that I have learned from making ads, coaching talents, and selling mostly meaningless stuff to people who did not even know they wanted to buy. Lessons that many of us know, or should have known or wished we had known . . . which, regardless, we largely ignore anyway . . . but it is these two basic tools: Verbal Communication and Written Communication.

Verbal communication provides boundless opportunity. It provides speed, intonation, and immediacy as some of its most significant advantages. Other benefits of verbal communication are, or can be, its emotionality, its one-on-one directness, and the human connection factor of being eye to eye, or the positive feeling derived from being heard or communicated with. It also packs the expediency to instantly fire words at will—geez, what a gift is speech? Most of us can be armed to launch a verbal onslaught in a moment's notice like a crazed man with a hair trigger and an itchy finger. The fact that we can speak nearly three times faster than the average person can write and comprehend is amazing, and environmentally friendly—and entirely worthless when the crazed man fires his mouth off before he thinks!

Being human, we possess an incredibly unique and fortuitous biological and physiological characteristic: our vocal cord infrastructure. Equally fortuitous was early man's ability to rapidly carve and craft a transformative language path that began with grunts and chest pounding and led to tweets and chest pounding in just a couple of hundred thousand years. In a geological quantum leap, we bridged and bridled our monosyllabic grunts and utterances with meaning, and contextualized them into vast agreements of understandings in no time.

Communication Breakdown

Written communication provides boundless opportunity, structure, and control of the message. Its permanency was a game-changer. History can be written. Treaties can be signed, and love letters can be sealed with a kiss and last forever. The special caveats of written communication can be both advantageous and limiting, interdependent upon its situational environs. While its permanence can deliver its message for all of its existence, its meaning can be interpreted with a high degree of variance. A "poison pen" can be deadly (meaning our words can be sharp and destructive), and it is also a two-edged blade (meaning your written word can come back to haunt you forever).

To query then, if my story about "THISlove" is a testimony of triumph for Verbal Communication, and my Cheerleader Love Letter to my son is potentially a testament to Written Communication, how is it we screw up so much of our communications today? To ponder this, can you think about your communications, both verbal and written?

Have you ever thought you have said too much? Too little? Do you forget what to say when you need to say it? Do you say too much, too often, to too many people? Have you regretted what you have said or written? Have you ever said, "Next time, I am going to tell them what I really felt"? Or "I should write a letter and tell them"? Or do you just stop talking? Are you one who wants to talk through everything, even in the middle of an argument or a fight? Do you find power in your words, or do you feel powerless when expressing yourself? Do you feel understood or otherwise respected in your opinions and points of views? Do you miss opportunity because of poor writing skills or fears of public speaking? Are you afraid to ask questions for fear of what others may think? Do you feel dominated by certain personality types? Do you despise small talk or incessant "talkers"? Can you tell one friend everything, and another friend nothing intimate or personal? Do you lie? Do you exaggerate? Do you listen for longer than sixty seconds? Do you think before you speak? Shall I go on?

There are so many beautiful stories told and to be shared—so many beautiful songs to play, to sing, and to write. So many arguments to resolve, fears to face, relationships to heal, businesses to lead, paths to forge, and chasms to close. And here you are stuck, stalled or stymied by words, meanings and understandings.

Our only hope for salvation lies in our ability to communicate. Our key to salvation is to empower the powerless and to encourage the disenfranchised to find their voice and re-script the conversation. That, and to raise their hand and speak up. Language is part of the game being played . . . and language has a storied past worth recounting.

You are
your word,
and it is
your world.

Like Humans Do!

My story and my recollection of the more recent history goes like this: The Sumerians started this whole written communication "business" barely 5,000 or 6,000 years ago and forever changed humanity. In an archaeological blink of an eye. We went from guttural utterances and cave paintings to the word processor and smartphone. And what do you get when you put guttural utterances and smartphones together? We get "Western thought"! Have you ever wondered why we think what we think? Could it be because it has been written down and said to you in rampant fashion as "what is so" with the world?

Allow me to hand you the lens by which to see exactly where we are now.

The Power of Perspective, Episode 3

Western thought stems from the time of Socrates, some 400 years before Christ. This was when our communications and thoughts were contextualized and written down, forever to be frozen and then handed down for the following 2,400 years or so. Imagine the pondering of the Greek philosopher Socrates, who was among the first to commit to writing some of his "greatest hits" of philosophy. It was from these writings that Socrates taught Plato. Then Plato, influenced from the writings of Socrates, created, morphed, formed, and committed even more thought to a lifetime sentence of remembrance, as he went on and taught Aristotle from those collective writings.

Would Socrates have believed that the art of communication would be forever changed, or become forever "frozen," by his use of the relatively new technology called "the written word"? I don't know, but then I think, "Did Louis Armstrong, Carl Perkins, and Chuck Berry expect Elvis Presley, The Beatles, and Pink Floyd to just sing covers of their originals?"

Look. The writings and philosophies of Socrates, Plato, and Aristotle are bedrock writings that much of modern thought today is built upon.

The Bible, the books of the Apostles, and their teachings of Jesus are bedrock writings that ALL modern Christian thought is built upon.

The Constitution, written by Thomas Jefferson, James Madison, with input from

John Adams and Benjamin Franklin, is the bedrock writing of our forefathers that ALL of our American laws today are built upon.

The writings of the Sumerians begat the writings of Socrates begat the writings of the Apostles begat the writings of Thomas Jefferson. Yet, since Socrates and the advent of Western thought, little has been added to the philosophical "thought train." Very little. The key word here being "added." However, today, the effects of these few writings, by these few men, are multiplied and compounded with incalculable outcomes.

Sure, Plato added deep thought and the development of political structure. Which was invaluable to society. And Aristotle added his deep thoughts, specifically the development of logic and science, which are the antecedents to our legal systems, deductive reasoning, and fields like biology. Also great.

And yes, further adjunct theories developed—no doubt. Again, the writings and words of Socrates, Plato, and Aristotle would later influence (ancient) philosophers such as Zeno and Marcus Aurelius, whose disciplines and learned virtues would become known as *Stoicism*, added everlasting thoughts on man's self-control, human tranquility, and his harmonious alignment to social independence. Today, the word "stoic," which is derivative to Zeno principle philosophies, defines one who holds fortitude without complaint.

Another man, named Epicurus, contributed profound thoughts and teachings about how a life worth living is the life that is spent seeking pleasure, indulgence, and social harmony—including music, literature, and art. The word "epicurean" comes from Epicurus. Epicurus also handed us the thought that many possible worlds can coexist, and that our world exists and occurs by chance, and therefore we should "enjoy the finest things" that our world can provide.

The last guy to know, for now, was named Pyrrho. He was super cool. He gave thought to the idea that freedom and happiness are only achieved when NO judgment exists; instead, man only needs to suspend doubt and replace it with a perpetual inquiry. Today, because of Pyrrho, we use the words "skeptic" or "skepticism."

So let's just say our Greek philosophers were great. Their ancient writings, thankfully, are ever present and available for review and analyses. But then again, they are two-thousand-year-old teachings. For two thousand years, most teachings of Greek philosophy were transferred from written word to spoken word. That is, the thoughts of thinkers became writings, and those writings were then taught and told to others, thus becoming a study of the others' thinking, then repeated ad infinitum.

Let's also agree that two thousand years ago, when writing was somewhat of new technology, a lot of people didn't read and write. Agreed? And while education was indeed spreading, along with political, legislative, and social control, the words that were spoken and transferred didn't change that much over time. Each generation learned old thoughts, not necessarily new thoughts. Our learning was, and is, sourced back to the original writings of Socrates, Plato, and Aristotle, therefore creating a "fixed thought" paradigm, perhaps for eternity.

The Printed Word Changed the Meaning of the Spoken Word

There's some beauty in that thought. There is some terror in that thought, too. Just think what the world would be like today if music was a "fixed thought" paradigm.

The Bible is a fantastic read—in English or any other modern language. But it was written in Ancient Hebrew, Aramaic, and Greek two-thousand-ish years ago, and roughly translated into agreeable meaning over and over. Wise words, but taught and retaught as antiquated parables. Again, a spoken story that roughly translated into the tale of Jonah living inside the belly of a whale for three days or Moses being six hundred years old as fact. But was it? How would you interpret it if someone said it to you, or instead if you read it in a book? For much of the time the Bible has existed, there has not been many copies of the Bible. Just very few, until the advent of the Gutenberg movable-type printing press in the 1400s. Printing the Bible in English began in the 1500s. And still, very few printings and no means of distribution. The stories were told and taught. And handed down.

Each subsequent printing, and language adaptation, slightly modified the message. Each translation, something new. Something different. Something threateningly new, enough to ignite heinous religious wars in the Middle Ages from the

Crusades, to the Inquisition, to the Thirty Years' War. Countless conflicts, still to this day, claim some antiquated assessment of a fixed thought. Take the United States Constitution, for example.

Our Constitution is more than 240 years old. Yet it has been amended only twenty-seven times. The last amendment was passed in 1992 (to change what we pay our politicians). Prior to that:

- The 26th Amendment, passed in 1971, lowering the voting age to 18
- The 25th Amendment, passed in 1967, dealt with the succession process for death of a president
- The 24th Amendment, passed in 1964, removed the poll tax
- The 23rd Amendment, passed in 1961, allowed residents of the District of Columbia to choose electors for presidential elections
- The 22nd Amendment, passed in 1951, limited presidential terms to eight years
- The 21st Amendment, passed in 1933, repealed the 18th Amendment prohibiting the consumption of alcohol
- The 20th Amendment, passed in 1933, dealt with extenuating circumstances in presidential and congressional terms
- The 19th Amendment, passed in 1920, gave women the right to vote
- The 18th Amendment, passed in 1919, outlawed the consumption of alcohol, which, as noted already, was repealed in 1933.

In one hundred years, just nine changes.

What's Going On?

In more modern times, Friedrich Nietzsche and Sigmund Freud contributed greatly in the 19th century to the "thought train." Nietzsche gave us sayings like "That which does not kill us makes us stronger." He also stated that his belief in and the use of "envy, alcohol, and religion" were all human weaknesses, limiting our greater potentials. He wrote: "How little you know of human happiness, you comfortable people." Living dangerously, and through difficulty, is indeed living.

Freud showed us what our neuroses may be, introduced us to psychoanalysis, and gave us thoughts on the pleasure principles. You know, the easy addictions and rewards of the physical and the emotional. Rewards like our oral fixations, our anal retentiveness, our phallic and sexual conundrums, and some throwback to a Greek tragedy called the Oedipus complex. Freud inadvertently provided us with the catchphrase prompt "penis envy!"

There is so much to consume from our ancestors, from the Greeks to the modern philosophers—man oh man, it's all wonderful, you know, if you look. All of it written down and handed down. Everything, from how to govern to how to worship. How to think and how to feel. How to conform, fear, doubt, control, and condemn. It's all there. Have you read it? Have you heard of it? Certainly, others have—and how's that been working for you? Are we only the sum total of what has now been written and said of us?

Well . . . THIS Is New

For most of the last few millennia, we have been told the stories of our existence. Told, because for most of that time, most people didn't read. That is still true to this day. I am just saying—I mean, come on—literacy is way up in the last two hundred years. Impressive work, y'all! But while today most people can technically read, they don't read to a saturated level of comprehension or retention. We still prefer to be told what we need to know. It is here we must focus our attention. To get THIS, we need to know this.

Today, our so-called smartphone society is booming. But so are our neuroses and anxieties—heightened to extremes. We are *woke* to our new heightened social awareness. More woke than we've ever been. Woke with technology. Woke with access to information. Finally, after two thousand years, an onslaught of new information is pouring in in untold millions of multiples. In 2017, YouTube reported that four hundred hours of video content was being added every minute. Google performs 3.8 million searches per minute. It is widely accepted that more information is uploaded and made available on Google and YouTube in just one day than was available in all of history prior to the advent of the internet. Yes, that is a lot of information. But is it information overload? No. In large part, the displacement of old information is by replacement of much new content and little new information. Information, nonetheless.

In a January 2017 *Psychology Today* article titled "The Effects of Digital Technology on Reading," Martin L. Kutscher, MD, reports "concern that the reliance upon shallow reading may interfere with the development of deep reading skills, such as thoughtful pondering, critical analysis and inferential thinking."

My "inferential" experience says that the absorption of information, the retention of information, remains unchanged by the average individual. Most Christians haven't read the Bible. They have been told its contents, its highlights, its essence. Or Socrates, for that matter. Pick any subject matter, and in general, we know a little about a lot. Most know just the "catchphrases" or "greatest hits," if at all. I, too, am among them. And like the average individual, I sense I am being swallowed by a "feeling of information overload," but more factually, "I am becoming less knowledgeable," less powerful, less hopeful, and more susceptible to control or manipulation.

I have pursued this journey enough to find that the key to enlightenment is my consciousness to think differently, and it is here that I may feel like Freud when he famously said, "The chief patient I am preoccupied with is myself." I was thinking of this when I wrote, "I share THISday because I am fixing me. I do this not to fix you. I can only share what I can share, then most humbly cheer for you. It is your life. Your game. Your song to write and your song to sing."

"No one who disdains the key will ever be able to unlock the door." A Freudian slip, this is not.

Yes, Thoughts become things, but it is our words that become our thoughts, feelings and choices.

The Grind

Look, we all get stuck from time to time. Some of us more than others. Some may not even know they are stuck. The fixed-thought syndrome that has us stuck is curable. But it is not a pill. Or a multistep process, or a meme. THISday is an idea. It is a juxtaposition of words, meanings, listening, understanding, and thought. And it may very well be a key for you to unlock a door. Though if it were, you would need to recognize it as a potential key. This means "getting it." Getting, having, knowing the information that I am sharing is in fact a potential key . . . and giving it a try. And, even if you get it, have it, and know it is the key, and you give it a try and it unlocks a door for you, you will still have to do a few more things. You will have to want to push open the door. You will have to want to go through the door. You will have to want to enter into a new space. You will want to willfully face the unfamiliar. You will need to leave the space you are in.

That's a lot of metaphor.

But then again, so is THISday. It is metaphor about thinking differently about how we approach the tough things in life. The important things in life. The littlest things in life. Whatever those things are to you.

The letter I wrote to my son is not a superhero "dad" letter. It's just one of the options out there—one of my voices, perspectives, and fortunate graces that I have acquired by THISlove and by understanding that I can have different thoughts. I can choose better words, different words, in order to evoke different and better outcomes. THISday happens when "expectation to outcome" gets dismissed from the conversation. It is nurtured when parties drop both expectation and outcome. Please don't get me wrong; setting expectations and outcomes is vital in human life, and the world in general, but should be blatantly expressed as agreement. Expectation, when laden in all of our conversations with our children, spouses, employees, et al., create undue or unintended pressure from some fixed thought.

So some people think, "Well, pressure creates diamonds!"

And others would argue, "Well, pressure causes explosions, too!"

Both are correct. But sometimes, when we communicate, we unintentionally apply pressure upon others.

Attachment to outcome dynamics are tricky. We use them every day, in virtually everything we do when interacting with others. We use them for needed results-oriented situations and agreements. We use them in need-seeking/obligatory (expected or anticipated) responses, like "fishing for compliments" or even with holiday gift giving, where there is this expected outcome. The give SO you get.

For example, if, a compliment to a partner such as, "You look nice today," were not returned by the other half, for example, "You look nice, too," the partner may be let down or have their feelings hurt.

There are a zillion other ways to handle this. What was really needed in the communication? Was there an outcome needed? If so, why not say so? If not, then think and choose your words better—because words matter. They build so many great things, when assembled appropriately and with thought. They cause wars, unintended problems, and undue pressures when not assembled with care and forethought.

Here I was dealing with my kid. And I chose differently. It was risky, because I had to get over my need for expectation and outcome. Situationally, he is a twenty-year-old man. Subjectively, I may or may not agree with that. The reality of it? I cannot change that, either. But I can create different conversations that may change a moment. A space that is more nurturing for greater outcomes over time. THIS love is what I seek, so THISlove is what I sow.

Listen, if you can be your WORD, then can you not be ANYTHING you want to be?

Five Questions to Ask Yourself

While sowing and reaping sounds logical, it is ultimately a fable, too. A pretty good fable, but a fable nonetheless. Reaping and sowing requires time, and involves many variables such as watering, weeding, and of course, harvesting. Reap and sow clichés do not produce predictive or immediate gratifications. And they do not remove my immediate worries or concerns that I held for my son. Moreover, these words then produce exploratory thoughts that we may consider as we enter our next challenging conversation:

1. At the intersection of THISmoment and you, who will you be?
2. At the intersection of THISproblem and you, who will you be?
3. At the intersection of THISday and you, who will you choose to be?
4. At the intersection of THISyear and you, who will you seek to be?
5. At the intersection of THISlife and you, who will you proclaim to be?

If you are your word, then can you not be anything? Thinking about these questions allows me to calm down and consider more wisely how my words can be better received and understood, as well as what impact they would have and which outcomes would result from those words. Choosing THISday, and its varied paths and potentials, did not remove my worries or concerns for my son. The words I chose did, however, change the probable outcome that the predictable and fallible speak of a discontented dad might have. The approach awakens you. It stirs the pot of possibility. That all sounds fine and fancy, but the truth of my courage was equally constrained by the chains of my vulnerability—I was a nervous wreck. Look, I took a risk. What dad was showing up for THIS kid? Yelling dad, with predictable and foretelling outcome. The Too Busy dad who was too busy to act like he cared. Of the dozen dads I could have created, I invented THISdad: I was vulnerable, open, fun, and expressive. I wasn't immovable, closed and shutdown, or a just a dick! Plain truth, thoughtfulness, and non-clingy caring showed up for a kid. Will he get it? Will he get the meaning, the understanding? In time, he certainly will. In his time.

In my time, so far, I have been able to release my attachment for outcome.

My son texted me the next morning, "Hey Dad. Read the email. Thanks. I needed that. You are a good writer. I'm good. I love you."

And for now all was perfect between us. It was always perfect. "I'm good." That's what I got. I didn't expect it. Whether I needed it or not, that was not on the table. It's what he decided to return to me. I didn't solve his problems. I didn't add to his problems, either.

When we need to have conversations about expectations and outcomes, we can. On this day, with THIS love, I changed both of our future outcomes potential . . . exponentially.

I know this because this was the night that bore my inspiration to share my voice with this world. And my kid is on a unfolding path, becoming the man he chooses to become without mixed messages from his dad.

Lyrical Lessons of THISlife

I don't always know the meaning of the songs I hear. Do you? I didn't think so.

If you are like me, you like music. Most people do. I love music and I am curious about lyrics, so I study them. I have studied them for more than forty years. It's like poetry. I am not entirely into poetry, but song lyrics move me. So that's poetry, right? Or is it just words smartly arranged for precise effect? Either way, lyrics have moved me throughout my life, and I am betting it has done so for you.

Sometimes, it is inexplicable how things turn out in our lives. I am a marketer by trade—an expert in radio and TV marketing and production. I am an owner of a Hispanic advertising agency, a talent coach, a former morning-show DJ, and an aging Division I football player, which all adds up to an interesting set of happenstances. Yet the reflection of things in my collected life's rearview mirror is just MY collection. My collection along an unintended path. They are just MY stories now. But along my path, I wasn't present to any "story-in-the-making." I was playing the game with each endeavor being simply something that revealed itself before me along the path. "Should I turn left, turn right, say yes, say no, take a risk, stay put?" How do we choose or navigate our paths? By feelings. By influence. By the vibe. Or by the book.

Some, I am guessing, navigate by the book. I didn't have the book. What book?

Life's Anthems

Looking back at my eleven-year-old self, that's all I was: a skinny, towheaded strand of feelings and influence openness. I loved my cat, my dog, my room, and my radio. I was influenced by my brothers to play football and listen to songs they said were cool. I made friends with kids in the neighborhood and at school, mostly by age, proximity, and some element of socioeconomics; I am sure we had so much in common, but we didn't know or think about that. We liked each other because we liked music, talked about music, and listened to music. We played music games, where I sang a bit of a song, then another kid had to sing another song, then a third kid decided which song was better. We rotated who judged the next round.

I walked home from school with the neighborhood kids, and we talked of starting a band, but none of us played instruments. Some of those same kids got instruments one Christmas. I didn't. I got a record player.

Some of those kids became musicians. Three of those kids started a rock band, and after high school they moved to Seattle and became rock stars. Legit rock stars.

I became what I became. I loved my record player. I bought albums. I read the lyrics on the album sleeves and listened to ENTIRE albums over and over.

THISday

Oh, so many magical words and lyrics! What did they mean? I mean, what did I understand them to mean? More importantly, why did the words so deeply move me? How was it that I remembered them when I heard the song and forgot them afterward?

Thank God for Unanswered Prayers

When I think back, I find so much cosmic coincidence or just dumb luck and good fortune in the crazy paths our lives find. As much as I tried to will and conform my life to the images of others, in the end, I just couldn't. I didn't have a guitar, so I couldn't be a rock star. I worked my ass off to make it as a professional football player, but things just didn't quite work out.

But I did make it into the radio business! Boy, that record player sure worked out to be a solid gift of a lifetime!

My first job after my college football career ended was selling ads on a country radio station. I was hungry. Literally having just fallen off the "free ride" and training table wagon that college athletes are privileged with, I had to suddenly learn the lost art of fending for, and feeding, myself. One's hunger will do miracles for a young person, or any person.

One day, I used that old record player story to tell a new story about how long and how much I loved music. I told that story, virtually by accident, to the athletic marketing director at my university. Her husband just so happened to be the general manager at the local radio station. Soon after I told that old story, and the new story, this whole 'nother story began.

I quickly learned that to do well—to sell—we had to come up with good ad ideas. Early on, I found that in radio, people don't buy "spots"; they buy ideas.

The Pre-Learned Me: "Hi. I was wondering if you would like to advertise on my radio station?"

Advertiser: "No, please go away."

Lesson learned.

The Learned Me: "Hi Mark, I hope your day is going well. And I hope business is good, too. Listen, I have been thinking a lot about your business an awful lot lately, and then I had this incredible, incredible idea. It was so good that I thought to write you a commercial that will totally explain this unbelievable idea, which I am almost certain you will love. Do you want to hear the great commercial I wrote for you?"

Advertiser: "Yes! When can you come by?"

Cha-ching!

I got it. Words matter. How you say things matters.

Not that I knew at the time, but this "Learned Me" was a chrysalis cocooned by what felt safe and secure to a young man wanting to be like the others, who wore new suits, donned nice shoes, and smoked the good cigarettes. My sales conformation was easy, in hindsight. "When they say this, you say that" word and phraseology mastering led me to fast-forward to becoming a well-formed, moneymaking . . . cliché . . . with nicer shoes.

How DO YOU Do It?

To do well in advertising and marketing mostly means we have to be able to communicate creatively. We have to write and create commercials that connect, influence, and transfer emotionality. We can only write and create AFTER we listen, learn, think, and understand the client, the product, and the market.

Some marketers nail it! Some marketers fail it. But in the final analysis, we are all marketing ourselves or some *thing*. Every one of us.

It is the same in life: to have certain successes, we have to think and speak in ways that connect, influence, and transfer emotionality and understanding. Often, we don't get it right the first time, every time, or anytime. Sometimes, it just takes, well . . . time! And to think and speak in ways that connect, we don't need the skills of a poet, a songwriter, or a shrink. We do, however, need to strive to figure out what stops us in our lives, which means we need to think harder, think differently, and listen to the point of understanding. I am talking about so much understanding (derived from listening) that we could teach, and not just repeat, what we heard or listened to. Professionally, we need to understand the complexities and nuances of virtually everything before we speak so that when we do speak, we know what we are saying. Personally, it seems as if we tend to accept much less formality in our speaking, but we somehow push more of the emotionality. This is one reason we love lyrics and music.

THISday

I believe music is much more than poetry set to catchy music. Much more! Long before you heard the song, someone had some complex thought, something to say, maybe something to get off their mind and perhaps share with someone else. It was an artist writing the lyrics to convey their feelings, then setting them to music. Will it connect? Will it be accepted? Or did it just need to be written or said?

Get the words Right...

   and the right thoughts will follow.

   and the right feelings will follow.

   and the right mind will follow.

   and the right body will follow.

   and the right spirit will follow.

   and the right people will follow.

What Are Words For?

Music is everywhere around us, repeating over and over, over time. Sometimes with thousands, or tens of thousands, of impressions in our ears. With songs, our brains attach quickly to rhythm, pitch, and beat. Our brains have done so for millennia. It's why our brains can recall a tune or song we haven't heard in decades and sing along with it as if we'd listened to the song yesterday. Music, indeed quite literally, moves us. In fact, as humans, we are the only species neurologically designed to do so. Music and song produce vibrations in cadence and rhythm that push sound (air particles) in unique patterns that are recognized differently than normal sounds of, say, water running through a stream, or the wind blowing through the trees and grass. Sound and sound variation awakens us, alerts us, and sets our brain on notice, on "record." And we get a special bonus by being human: When sound hits our ears, we can instantly tap our feet to the beat, with no thinking required. Oh, and we can dance! Again, the only species to do so. Music and Song, Sound and Dance are special gifts to humanity.

Words are, too.

Although, communication (as an organized means to communicate, warn, and emote) is not exclusive to humans. Bears, whales, birds, trees . . .they all have communication, just as we do. Perhaps we are much more specialized, which may be debatable. Regardless, words, and the formation of human language and communication, were a massive social contribution to evolution and a necessity for human survival. They still are today, and I would like to believe they are still evolving. But we have some challenges with words. Spoken words can be forgotten. Just ask your significant other. Written words can last forever but need to be read again to be fully recalled. Words that are sung are perhaps better recalled because of cadence or syncopation. For example, if I read the numbers "8-6-7-5-3-0-9" to you out loud, most would get that I was giving you some numbers to remember, then you would promptly forget them. But if I sang "8-6-7-5-3-oh-ni-uh-ine," some would be like, "Jenny, Jenny, who can I turn to?" and sing the popular '80s song by Tommy Tutone.

Words matter. And we can't always sing them, or put them in a meme, or recall them. We forget them. Some words when spoken put us to sleep, like my college history professor so efficiently did to me. When some people try to communicate, it just comes out like a Charlie Brown cartoon moment when the teachers' talk goes: "Mwa-mwa-mwa." What did the "mwa-mwa-mwa" even mean?

And that's perhaps my ultimate, main point: What do the words mean? Words can have multiple meanings. Endless meanings. Changed meanings. Lost meanings. Miscommunicated meanings, where I meant one thing, and you interpreted it with another meaning. Word delivery matters, too. There is a distinct difference in meaning when I say, "Stop," and not, "*STOP!*" Just saying a word softly or shouting it, or with a voice intonation such as "Stopppppp," conveys different meanings.

Love Songs, or The Blues

I was singing at the top of my lungs to Clint Black in my truck—in Hollywood, California—a cover of The Eagles' "Desperado." Why my tears were streaming down my
cheeks while I sang this song for the nine hundredth time, or the nine thousandth time,
I did not know. I couldn't quite grasp the emotion so immediately. But then it hit me.
Was Clint right? Was I out riding fences for too long? The lyrics slapped me in my face
as I listened. As I heard. As I finally got what this song had been saying all this time!
My self-inflicted "prison" was "walkin' through this world totally alone, by choice. Man,
it hit me. It scared me. It got me. Finally! THIS tremendous "aha" moment. BAM! It fell
over me. Without a moment's delay, I called the girl I had just broken things off with
in El Paso, Texas, and begged her forgiveness and asked her to take me back. One
month later she moved in with me. Two years after that, THIS girl, she married me. No
kidding. We married November 11, 2011. Her name is Gaby. Don't worry, she thinks
this story is bullshit, too. But it is not. And yes, that's right: 11-11-11.

It's 11:11, Do You Know Where Your Angels Are?

In 2004, I somehow woke-the-fuck-up. The life that I'd lost during the divorce was not a life I regret losing, for it was a life that I can sparsely remember today. As I busied my single life to appear unaffected by all the doom, the pain, loss, and potential shadow the divorce might cast on my looking good among society, I did all of the things I had been meaning to do during my conformity years. In doing so, my supposed trans-formation was yet a mere re-conformation to what others would have me be: I lost weight. Dressed better. Got a pretty girlfriend. My being was: "Look at me. That Didn't Hurt."

This was not the wake-up call. Although, had it not been for the divorce event, I would still be fat and numb. The shiny new life was just that, shiny. Polished. I was just thinner. Missing my kids and still, unknowingly numb. And 11:11 was in high gear, now appearing as if it were in cahoots with a flashing neon-sign maker. It was flashing big and bright throughout my life.

My 11:11 experience turned exploration only after my fancy of the occurrences I now found amusing. I would tell stories of 11:11, and the oddities of their spooky and random appearances in my daily life. People likely thought that I was partly being chatty and partly being nuts. But it was a story . . . with odd and funny parts. I wouldn't ever fly on the SWA Flight 1111 between El Paso and Dallas, for it surely meant I would meet my doom. And the guy that lived at the 1111 address now dated my ex.

1111 was the fixation to justify my circumstance, my rightness, in a funny, ooky-spooky story that I would tell over and over. That story was a hit . . . I thought.

I did find one fan of that story; it was a woman I had dated, who texted me: "Google 11:11 now." Google wasn't the household name or go-to search tool in 2005, as it is today. Still, with one click, hundreds of results popped up for 1111; and I was reborn. I was re-scripted.

Like any newborn, I still didn't know much more than from the minutes earlier when I was still inside the womb. But something changed. There was a shift in my universe. And it was delivered in just a few words that read: "You have a purpose. You have a mission. You are an angel."

But what does a self-centered follower of the uninformed say when they get told they are an angel? Well, I said, "Hmmm . . . how weird. Cool!" And I went about my day.

The Soundtrack of My Life

Another tune I sang often went:

I am older now, my job rules my life

seems no time to do what I want to do with life, kids, or wife,

I'm stuck

or I'm threatened by things hard to see

feelings of another way I can just be

me the more I move ahead

seems the more I get behind

the games that they're playing,

the words that they're saying,

puts me at the end of the line.

I have listened and I have heard,

need to find the right word

for this life to change,

stop following the herd.

I wrote those lyrics. It's my pang song. While I haven't composed a melody for those lyrics, I have sung this song for years. Or at least, those words were my anthem of life. If only I knew how to play a catchy riff, or hold a melody, we could all sing the words half-right, for years, not really knowing what was being said, or what it meant.

THISday

If while reading my lyrics you struggled with trying to figure out exactly what song it was, or who wrote it, then you are wired perfectly to pursue understanding. If only when communicating and exchanging our innermost feelings . . . we tried with the same intent. To understand everyday conversations and communications.

So many songs (and conversations) to be discovered, rediscovered, and pondered; so much meaning to absorb. But will we not be the better for doing so?

Understandably, most songs have a very deep meaning to the artist, yet likely evoke a much different meaning, if any at all, to the listener. Many times, music and song can and will pose recollection of a time in our lives or a personal memory, and that is awesome. They can also make and create different meanings over time.

Is THIS Thing On?!

There exists massive variation in sound, songs, words, and meaning. But let's lean in on the recall and effectiveness (or actionability) of our words, both spoken and received. Again, through music as our metaphor, our words, both spoken and received by our brain, coupled with our recall ability and effectiveness (or actionability) of those words, have given us our position in life. Our place in the game. In other WORDS, you are where you are today because of things said and heard, and the feelings and meanings of those things said and heard, what those things said and heard really meant, and what you believed them to mean. You are where you are by choice. By accepting words, both used and received. You are likely not helpless. You are likely not a victim. You are likely not stuck. Your words (said and heard) can affect the position in life that you and others hold. When your words (said, heard, and believed) change, your position changes, your view changes.

Please don't act like you understand that if you don't. Read it again. I did, just to make sure from my end of the communication that these assemblies of words could make sense to a reasonable person on the receiving end of THIS communication. This is a lot like life, where something is said and you think you got it—enough—so you blow by it all in order to keep up. Maybe it's my writing? Not clear enough? Too much eighth grade for you? Not enough? The words we speak and receive come this way, too—simpatico or not simpatico. We do the same when people talk: Our brains are in a hurry—and we can lose track of a conversation. We jump ahead, or we anchor on a word, or we check out—and we don't listen. Again, in this world, words matter. But for words to matter, we must say listening matters. We have been hearing these songs for years—generations, even. We have been surrounded by this from all genres of music. Within moments, we can sing along to a song. That's amazing. But I can't remember the name of that person I just met.

So, did you hear the words? Or just the song? Did you get the meaning of the art being performed for you? The story given? The lesson of another's experience? Did you feel the pain, the fraught concerns of life, the profound message being shared?

Me neither, at first. But here's the thing: We hear just fine, but we often don't listen too well. Think about it. When you're in conversation with another person, are you really listening to what they're saying, hearing and thinking and emotionally reacting to their words? Or are you processing only on the periphery of the conversation, just waiting to jump back in and speak?

I am not judging. It's just this thing we do. Say "Hi" to your ego!

If I believe in you,
that means you
and I have believed
your words.
If I don't believe
in you it is because
I have not.

Form Dictates Content

That's how it goes with words, poetry, and lyrics; once written, sung, or spoken, they often reveal linear meaning for a brief moment of clarity or understanding before being closed like a book, overcome by the beat and guitar solo, or simply forgotten.

Words are like that. Poetry is like that. Songs are like that. They are drowned out, sealed shut, or tucked away in the recesses of our minds. If these are our words and conversations that are drowned out or forgotten, what now?

If our goal is to pursue understanding, then a different approach, for a different sense of what is communicated is needed or needs to be present. While more rhetoric is spun, and more poetry is written, and more music is undoubtedly produced, our depth of listening must constantly be retuned, retrained, and required for building new foundations of meaning and understanding. For without, our conversations and interactions with other humans will be devalued and lose continuity. We may lose or miss out on clarity. If we can accomplish this task, our relationships with kids, parents, co-workers, lovers, communities, politicians, friends, and adversaries would, therefore, be different, and potentially better, wouldn't they? Yes! The answer is yes, if we care enough to express ourselves with more intent of being understood.

Oh Lord, Please Don't Let Me Be Misunderstood

I am continuously moved by composers, musicians, and singer-songwriters who make lyrics come to life. I love their commitment and willful vulnerability to express themselves, to have their music heard, understood, and judged, as they persevere through innumerable obstacles to get these messages to us. Many artists sacrifice greatly for years, just to get us to listen. But many of us just hear the melody and miss the pain and emotion expressed.

Are we open to receive the word, the meaning, or the understanding? Are our channels tuned to "listening with purpose to understand"? Or not.

There are so many wildly different nuances to absorb. We claim to love their stories. We claim to love the life struggle expressed and shared. The love of music and lyrics seems so common, as common as not listening while hearing.

I guess that's the thing. We hear songs over and over and miss the point of the message.

Is that not the same with our words? Is that not the same with our conversations?

In THIS moment, we can see what we have learned is learned by what we have heard, listened to, and have understood. THIS reveals a new understanding. Here, we get an idea that perhaps we have missed a few things communicated and shared with us, time and again, with people we love, with people we work with. And the people we argue with. In music, we see and hear the artistry of words, varied meanings, and soul-bearing attempts to connect, human to human. What do we see and hear in our daily conversations?

Are your words heard, honored, and understood as soul-bearing attempts to connect human to human?

Do you hear and honor and understand the words of another attempting to connect with you?

Our comprehension of "understanding and meaning" must evoke our intent. Our intent is the act of listening. Our listening needs to be made present and actively engaged.

The Loving Understanding Perspective of Ignorance, Hate, and Prejudice

As I comprehend "UNDERSTANDING," it is merely the power derived from abstract thought and awareness. This includes all shades of things like perception, judgment, sympathy, awareness, perception, and point of view. Oh, and do I need to mention that they all require listening *and* articulation?

Another way to pinpoint understanding is to define its opposite. The opposite of understanding is ignorance. I'm not sure how "ignorance" became such an offensive word, but think of this more like the word "ignore." So, not so much as in the word "dumb"—but more like forgetting to "care" about understanding one another or understanding another's point they were trying to make.

The significance of "MEANING," on the other hand, is more akin to things like interpretation, essence, significance, definition, or explanation. MEANING tends to relate more to the intentions of the person who communicated the words, whereas UNDERSTANDING relates more to the perceived awareness of another's communicated words.

Look, I understand that both meaning and understanding get thrown around a lot in every conversation. And the two are often interwoven in conversation as being synonymous, which technically they are not; but they are.

THISday

Love and hate, and our multifaceted prejudices or diatribes eke into our vernacular at a fevered, breakneck pace. The pressure to like/love/hate our world's offerings is the calling of our social experiments via social media. Truncation of expression, down to a single emoji, has us pining for a basis of acceptance from a world that is finding interpersonal relationships ever-so-elusive without dropping a WTF or LOL into our sentences—that is, if we were actually talking with someone, you know, with voices and all.

The time—so precious—of real and heartfelt words may be escaping us and being replaced by SMS-type characterization of what we mean to say . . . only to be misinterpreted or lost in the rampant noise of our verbal, auditory, and intellectual assault. The dumbing down of society, full of loaded and leveraged words, half meanings, double entendres, or cynical word traps. Traps so easily set, yet escapable for any person to "talk their way out of owning them." Is there such a perspective any longer that trusts a man or a woman "at their word"?

One way to know if you are "playing the game" is to know that you are playing a game with your word—that you have command of verbal variations as sport. Let's call it what it is: Texting emojis is fun. It breaks the ice and adds new twists to the game. It is, however, not a game if you cannot switch it off, and your poor—and possibly ignorant—communications communicate poorly and full of ignorance. Assumptions of meaning, word traps, and cynicism can both create a kingdom and burn one down.

Look, it's often one word, the last word, the unfiltered word that ignites the fight. It's the slip of the tongue, the absence of mindfulness that breaks the bond, loses the deal. It is the phrase that is repeated in our prayers, in our meditations, or in our interactions that does allow us to connect at levels needed to advance our thoughts, feelings, and spirit. Over time, our lost communicative efforts create voluminous spaces in our hearts and our minds that get filled with negative experiential outcomes. Not winning, loss, loneliness, and depression can fill those voids, a word at a time, creating vast oceans of broken words and negative thought. And negative feelings. Negative outlooks.

Word games are fun only when we win.

*Symptoms are
to Cure what
Thoughts are
to Words*

Sensing Perspective

Listening is a sensory thing. Like seeing, tasting, smelling, touching.

When we smell something . . .

When we touch something . . .

When we taste something . . .

When we see something . . .

We first identify. We match. We sort. We source. We ingest. We determine. We savor. When we hear something, it's a bit different. With sound. It's primal. Unlike our other senses, our sound sensory never rests. We can close our eyes and not see. We can shut our mouths and not taste. We do not always smell. And we are not always sensing touch.

But listening is different from hearing. This very moment, I am present to my hearing. The keyboard clicks. Street noise. The heater. The hearing sensory is always on. However, I called my listening into the present. Now my awareness of hearing is heightened. And I can now actively identify, match, and sort the source of what I heard. That presence I called into my hearing sensory—that's called listening. But there's more.

While I now have the sorted identification and source of my listening, I must continue to accelerate my listening state to "active listening" to maintain the flow of more information. This active listening allows for elective sorting. Once here, I can consciously make decisions for things like actions needed, short-term or long-term retention, mental imprints, or recording and understanding.

It is here where we make mistakes. It is here where we inadvertently assert meaning ahead of understanding. With music, our sensory works almost automatically. We tap our feet to the beat quite subconsciously. We sort and source and determine our liking or enjoyment of the hearing. We may recall, magically, the beat. We may have heard this song a thousand times. But we may only have a small understanding of the words, much less their meaning. Our recollection of the song may have more of an imprint of a personal memory—a sentimental attachment to when the song and some other occurrence combined. Therefore, the song may make you happy or sad. It may cause you to reflect fondly of times past. Of people and friends. Moments, images, feelings. It's powerful. But having melodies prompt our memories does not mean we understand the song, or more specifically its words, message, and meaning that the artist wrote and intended. Hearing the song and understanding the song are wildly subjective points of experience.

In everyday conversations, understanding words, for example in a sentence, is paramount. Assigning meaning is subjective.

The intended meanings of the words are ONLY available from the source of the words. The interpretation of words is personal and subjective. What this song means to me, what it means to you, and what it means to the artist are three different things. Each of those meanings are neither right nor wrong. They are just meanings assigned to words and the assembly and orchestration of the words.

The understanding of the words assembled in music and in life is essential. Our

130

ACTIVE LISTENING is the only thing that can get us to UNDERSTANDING. After we understand, we can each individually assign meaning. Many times, we interchange words like "hearing" when we mean "listening." So we often spend our time clarifying:

- What's that about?
- What's he saying?
- How'd he say it?
- That's what I meant.
- What does that mean?
- So, what you're saying is . . . ?
- I'm confused.
- I thought he was saying . . .

Hey, Children, What's That Sound

Anytime you are ready to test listening, find some songs that you love to hear, along with the lyrics to read. Then listen and read along with the words. Concentrate and read them as they were first written—as if it were poetry.

After you listen and read, you can ask yourself what you learned. What opened up for you? What is new in your understanding of the words said when listened to differently and with intent? This is the process of THISday. Now that we can see differently, we can seek differently. Now that we can hear differently, we can know differently. This is the learning to learn, while unlearning egocentric listening, thought-anchoring, and auditory absence.

We have been hearing these songs for years—generations, even. We have been surrounded with this from all walks of life. Sometimes, in the "real world," music is just noise that fills emptiness. Other times, the guitars may drown out the meaning of the lyrics and we may miss the message. Just like the noise of our parents' voices drowned out their message. Or our boss's noise. The noise coming from the TV. Noise from cars/airplanes/trains.

Word redundancies, unfocused noise from crowds, and the deafening volumes in our AirPods make us, at times:

- Lose the point or importance of things
- Lose the meaning of things
- Get our priorities messed up
- React or behave erratically
- Stop listening
- Slow to learn
- Seek a different beat to tap our feet to

Sometimes, even when we feel we are listening, we:
- Misinterpret what is being said
- Think it means something else
- Hear the wrong word (but sing it anyway)
- Forget the words
- Just go along with it because everyone else does
- Again, we hear just fine. We just don't listen too well.

When we don't listen well, we miss the meaning, the message. We miss out on what's most important. We miss the opportunity be eloquent and simple with words. Poetic, even. Well-chosen, well-expressed words change the world. Like a great song, our words can last. Especially when the words we are listening to are our own.

The Needle Is Stuck

The best words orchestrated, enunciated, and expressed with consideration and compassion communicate best. But sometimes they simply miss their mark. Say one thing truthful and right, complimentary and kind, just once and you may be rewarded for a day. Say all things right from THISday evermore and be rewarded for a lifetime. Sometimes we don't express ourselves well. It happens to everybody. That's what was euphemistically termed "a failure to communicate."

But our words can unstick us as easily as they can stick us. They can move us, inspire us, and create our world or tear it down. Knowing how to collect and conjure words from our successful and failed attempts in the circle of communication is an enviable skill set. And to think that you cannot improve that skill set—or to not even consider improving that skill set—is ultimately debilitating. To dismiss the importance of improving your language is to dismiss the validity of your thoughts and your feelings. It is to dismiss the very mind-body-soul-spirit-feeling-healing systems, as each are exclusively dependent upon words and what you make them mean. Words constitute thoughts and evoke feelings. Our feelings sanction our ego, and then our ego sanctions our feelings. If your language is garbage, then so are your thoughts and your feelings and all the systems that culminate into making you the you that you are.

Getting unstuck is dependent upon our ability to hone word usage to improve our message, our song, our story—apart from ego. What our language can teach, do, and create for us is invaluable. Language is key to our emotional happiness. When we stop learning to advance our communicative abilities, our verbal skills atrophy. A disease of language can fester. Chronic ignorance, chronic stupidity . . . yes, you have seen it. It runs rampant. Untreated, it causes people to repeat words and reach for toxic adverbs that don't measure up to the word choices that could have changed the message, or the moment. Egocentric and ill-placed terms like "always" and "never" and "hate" are early symptoms of the disease. "You are ALWAYS late" and "You NEVER look at me anymore" are absolute indications of poorly selected and applied words. They can be so divisive to healthful communication. "I 'hate' strawberries," or "I 'hate' . . . any-thing," is such blatantly absurd usage that it renders the speaker ineffectual to anyone of higher language capabilities. Feckless to compete. Toothless, while armed with a social media account.

And here we are, stuck in a world of chronic stupidity running amok. It sickens me that the truth needs to be shocking and that we consider a lie as valid expression of normal, everyday communication. Really? Am I crazy?

Get the words Wrong...
   and the wrong thoughts will follow
   and the wrong feelings will follow.
   and the wrong mind will follow.
   and the wrong body will follow.
   and the wrong spirit will follow.
   and the wrong people will follow.

How Hard Can THIS Be?

I so clearly remember playing on my grandparents' farm, trying to get the freshwater-well pump to produce a consistent flow of water. In those days, well pumps were a simple siphoning apparatus that provided us with our entire water supply for cooking, drinking, and so on. If you've ever tasted the freshness of earthen well water reborn from deep beneath the Midwestern soil, then you know that the pure, chilling, crisp taste of a single drop makes it worth all the effort. But my frantic pumping was using every ounce of my strength; I was producing more sweat drops than water drops into my cup! I pumped that handle for what seemed to be a million times and was still not able to get the water flowing enough to fill my little paper cup. Even though I had raw effort and determination, I still had an empty cup.

Soon after my near collapse, my father arrived with a five-gallon stainless steel bucket and placed it under the spigot. He grabbed the pump handle and gave it the same action I had given the handle but with a fraction of the effort, and the well pump quickly shot full volumes of cool, crisp water into his bucket. It took my father just seconds to fill the whole bucket to the top. He wasn't even out of breath!

How could the process of gathering water be so easy and rewarding for one and fruitless and exhausting work for another? "Really, how hard can THIS be?"

We had no lakes or rivers nearby. No easy access to surface waters. Our water was underground. And I am sure, before the advent of the well pump, I would have caravanned water a hundred miles. In truth, if gathering water weren't so darned necessary to sustain life, we may not have tried pumping water ever again! But trying harder was not the answer. And Lord knows I tried.

My father explained that "trying harder" isn't the solution to achieving more. Sometimes, it's a big part of the problem. He said, "If you stake your hopes of getting what you want on just trying harder than ever, you may kill your chance to succeed." He took the time to show me the technique required to get water from the well, and it was the simplest thing to do. I worked a lot less, and I got lots of water.

Once my father showed me how he operated the well pump, I didn't have to practice, working my way up little by little, to produce the same results. I simply let go of my old ways and followed a known method of success and abundance. For me, it was a quantum leap in effort and results.

Thirst vs. Abundance

I am still perplexed, and somewhat humored, by this anecdotal experience of mine when I observe friends and business owners exclaim, "I tried it once, and it didn't work!" Meanwhile, other people and businesses are growing abundantly wealthy by doing the very thing other people and businesses said didn't work.

Perhaps it is okay for some folks to survive on the drops of sustenance that their "given-up" attitude provides. But I know this, being "thirsty" can make for busy work.

Working with "thirsty" folks is very frustrating. They will try anything once and move on. They passively listen and look for the next big "thing" that will get them to abundance. These are the ones who keep digging for their water everywhere, trying this spot and that spot, and never breaking through. Said another way, these are the people who continuously dig one-foot wells a hundred times over, instead of digging a one-hundred-foot well one time! It's the same amount of digging, right?

I Can't Explain

THIS isn't about water. This is a distinction many often miss or seldom get. THIS story is about work, friends, love, time, life, and making a difference by creation of our actions. When we learn, the effort becomes effortless. It is the same with talking, listening, learning, and understanding. It's not about trying or working harder. Working hard is for the uninformed and the "unwoke." If we can unlearn that hard work equals success, and acknowledge that all work is just that . . . it's work. Listening is work, and so is understanding. Love and friendships and life in general can be so hard for some, and effortless for others.

"My Arrow,
I assure you,
spares one.
You will all dance
to the ballet of
which I sing."

– The Danse Macabre

F*ck You, Fate

Fate did NOT bring us together . . . Our words have. Words, thoughts, and the seismic SHIFTS we can leverage with our mindful perspectives—that is what brings us together.

No matter your position, your station in life . . . our lives are full. Full of expectation and have-tos and unfulfilled intentions . . . some good, and the others, well, haplessly maligned. But, as we aspire to become more and more awakened—and we are—we become aligned or confronted with these facts: We must know and acknowledge that right now, this very moment, we are here together because of some FANTASTIC set of circumstances that we have called for and that we have manifested. Own your circumstances, past and present.

Those fantastic circumstances, at the core, are the result of our words, of our thoughts, and of what we have chosen those words and thoughts to mean. It is ULTIMATELY a personal choice . . . judged by YOU, not your parents, your partner, your neighbor. You choose your life because you choose the words and the thoughts, and therefore you choose the outcome. You choose your circumstances. You are neither victim nor hostage to them, though . . . they are NOT your fate.

Too often fate is portrayed as a mystical, supernatural, and enigmatic occurrence or realm of circumstances that gets pawned off as destiny because the explanation of the FATEful happenstance is too wild or unexplainable. Or perhaps words can't do it justice. *"You don't understand."* Or: *"You would have to see it to believe it."* Or: *"You're never going to believe it."* Or: *"It was just FATE."*

But it IS explainable. And there is a path we can pursue to understand our "fate." Whichever words you choose to believe, mine or others, know there is much more to pursue. Here is but one explanation/belief . . . It is *amor fati*. That is Latin, and in Stoic philosophy translates as *"a love of one's fate.*"

That means the most resolute and enthusiastic acceptance of everything, most specifically death.

Amor fati means there is neither melancholy nor mystery for things that happen in our lives . . . GOOD or BAD . . . that there is simply acceptance of what is—WITHOUT requiring meaning—acceptance with a matter-of-factness, and acceptance with gratitude for that fact.

Stoics see *amor fati* as singularly virtuous, because the only fate there is—the one we all must face—is ultimately the most fatal: death. The virtue comes from seeing death as acceptable and inarguably fateful.

Everything else that you may think of as fate is, arguably, not.

What stirs the cosmos, the universe, and Twitter-verse, is all the same . . . but it is not fate. It is our words and thoughts that we put forth into the world, and nothing more. And what becomes of those words and thoughts, and how they manifest themselves *or* what is returned to us and others can be so special and seemingly divine. Is it Karma? Destiny? Free will? Serendipity? Luck, either good or bad? Who knows for sure? But fate it certainly is not.

In full and fair measure, what is returned from our words—the products of our

143

THISday

thoughts, whether those thoughts and words are good OR bad—is and forever will be equally abundant. Choose good words, choose good thoughts, and have a positive acceptance of everything.

Do this THISday, and every day until your last day, because fate will undoubtedly have the last word with us all. Until then, all the words are ours.

F*ck you, fate. You'll have to wait.

The hardest thing about enlightenment is that Hypocrisy hates confrontation.

A Letter of Disparate Love to My Republican Brother

You can choose to have a brother or no brother. A sister. A parent. Or to not. We absolutely do not need them. If you want one, get one. Blood or no blood.

I have plenty of brothers. Blood brothers, band-of-brothers, big brothers, brothers-from-other-mothers, and brothers-in-arms. I just wanted *this* brother back, the brother from *my* mother.

To keep this brother, if I had any say in the matter, and I did, I would rather bite my tongue then speak ill of him. Or if I had no better words to enhance a conversation—I'd keep my mouth shut. But I love my brother, and I wanted to strangle him.

In recent conversations, my brother and I had had too many nonproductive discussions about politics over the phone and text, and they were escalating from conversations to full-blown "FU" fights. I am not a believer that people should avoid talking politics, religion, or any subject matter—to anyone. But political conversations are particularly tough. Political conversations featuring interruptions, elevated voices, short answers, unsubstantiated claims, false narratives, satirical memes, and emojis are guaranteed to bear no fruit—and to produce a lot of thorns. I love my brother, and I loved debating him about anything. Politics had been our main course for months and months now. And the political and verbal banter had taken a turn for the much worser.

Every conversation started with a "Hey man, what's up?" and ended with an f-bomb and click. It was not working at all anymore. Not via phone, text, or email.

Because sometimes saying nothing speaks volumes, and sometimes saying nothing makes you complicit, this seemed like an excellent opportunity to do something—anything—to get us on track. So, I wrote. And I wrote. And then I wrote:

Just What We Needed – a letter

July 2018

Brother Tim,

I am hoping that by writing you a letter, quite possibly the first "real letter" in our lifetime, we will accomplish a few positive things in our brotherly, loving, needing, and supporting relationship.

Perhaps it will be a better understanding of things between us. This letter is vital to me. Maybe it will allow you and I to slow down enough to write and/or read something that takes careful thought and focus to actually "get." Or not. But I will try to say what is in my heart.

It has been fifty-plus years of brotherhood, and we have collected many things in this relationship. It is easily understood and normal that from my point of view, I harbor and hold dearly my experiences of our relationship. I harbor my opinions. I harbor my thoughts and memories. Good and bad. While I have burned many of the negatives, I have equally framed the positives, and I permanently retained millions of wonderful, silly, unbelievable, perhaps even illegal, and yet deeply profound memories and experiences that are uniquely "ours." Unmovable pillars that have built me, my life, and my relationship with you, and, quite honestly, it is what completes me.

We are now two very grown men. Grown men with shared genes, parents, brothers, friends, girlfriends, cousins, clothes, experiences, traits, jobs, vacations, senses of humor . . . and on and on. It's enviable, no doubt. And it's ours! It gives us, us!

As with all that we have in common, we are wildly different, too. That is totally awesome. Our differences, our identities, our distance from oneanotherness (a new word) make us better together. And the Lord knows, there shouldn't be two of us!

So this remarkable brotherhood, this totally idolized relationship, this unique thing we have, gets thrown up against whatever is going on in our lives. This has happened throughout our entire lives. We fought as kids, and we were extraordinarily mean to one another. Later, we have celebrated, been drunk and amazingly high, supported, and been loving to one another. We have cried, competed, and complained together. This carousel will continue.

We talk just to connect. To stay connected. We talk to fill our voids and to replenish our souls. I love that. We scheme ideas. We laugh. We are crazily crass, crude, and critical. Our humor is sick with cynicism and wrought with addictive giddiness. It only exists because of our collective investment of brotherhood. A place where one comment, one word, one glance, one lyric, or one gesture can communicate, accentuate, and authenticate our connectedness.

We spent years together and years apart. Neither has strained our relationship. More precisely, it has forged us to be stronger. It has furthered our experience together.

We spent years engaged in introspective talk, debate, and senseless rhetoric about everything: jobs, money, diets, kids, girls, politics, family, trips, and stupid drama. We have railed on so many things. We have challenged one another in thought

149

and action. We get that we can see things differently but find commonality. And we can be excruciatingly hard on one another.

Yet I find now that we truly exist in two very different bubbles. We all do. And we need to work to continuously recognize this, and work to pop these bubbles. In many ways, we didn't purposefully choose our bubble. It is just where we are presently.

At our core—or at least at my core—I (we) have a belief system that is not new for me (or us). But many times, things get tested with situational variance and/or justifications. For example: I don't hunt. I really don't like it. Why? Because I don't like killing animals. But I would likely kill someone if they hurt someone in my family. Wouldn't you? I once killed a bird and I regretted it. It made me sad. I like fishing, but not eating fish. I eat beef. But I hate the whole idea of killing cattle. I kill scorpions every day. No remorse. I believe in abortion rights for women AND I believe in the death penalty. Yet I don't advocate for abortion rights, and I would not want my wife or daughter to have one. If some family member of ours were convicted of murder, I really would expect them to be put to death but would fight like hell to keep them alive. I would break up a fight. I would stand up to a bully and have many times. I did it for you, a couple of times. I would risk my life to fight and/or save someone. I would report abuse (and have done so).

I give money to the homeless. I wish I could do more. But I don't think I would let them stay at my house. I pray to God, but don't go to church and often question the existence of a creator, and I don't believe in religion. Killing in the name of religion is just killing. But I raised my kids within the church. Go figure.

I think we became who we are today by way of our parents, our experiences, our stories we made up, and our rackets we have.

From there, we have surrounded ourselves with "what is important to us," according to what is in proximity to our bubble. What gets inside our bubble is up to us. It could be delivered there by the daily news. A neighbor or a friend's opinion. Science, or a new discovery you have learned about. Or perhaps by influence of the work we do. But it only gets in our bubble if you allow it to, or if it passes your "Smell Test." Does it match your preconceived beliefs, or counter your opinions? Yes, or no? In the bubble, or out?

But what we judge upon, we have no experience with personally. For example, we haven't faced a murder conviction in our family, a forced family separation, or a need to evacuate our homeland to save our lives. We don't make minimum wage, and we are not wage suppressed, at least I don't think we are. No one tells us what we can do with our body. We barely see our white privilege, likely due to our poor beginnings, but we know we have it. Right?

We are arguably hypocritical. We are fully judgmental. Many times, we are political oxymorons. Where do we fit in the modern political spectrum? High income, white, borderline boomers, reasonably educated, divorced, experienced in single parenting, struggling to get ahead. We have had our tough times but somehow got through it.

But those facts help forge our bubble. It creates a lens by which stupid words spill out, like "Geez, why can't others get through their hard times, like we did?" or "Slavery ended 150 years ago, right? Get over it!" or "I believe in personal responsibility to one's problems."

Sound familiar? Are we walking contradictions or are we just ignorant hypocrites? Are we complicit to our biggest issues, or are we just complacent. Because with every word I write, I hear my voice in clear contrast to my actions.

THISday

Well, here's the deal: We are not Black. We didn't start 300 years behind the rest of America. We didn't lose our jobs and our houses in the last recession. Our company didn't take a loophole and eliminate our entire factory. Our country didn't suddenly erupt into civil war and force us to move into refugee camps. Our kids aren't picked last. No one is sick in our family or has $3,000 per month in medical needs. Your kids' school wasn't shot up by a crazed gunman. So while we may try to empathize with these things when we see or hear about them, we have no firsthand experience or active experience with any of this. Yet we judge. We dismiss. We forget about who helped us out when we were down . . . then we say, "Oh, wow, that's horrible." Followed by, "What's for dinner? Oh, let's go out." Then we further dismiss this by thinking, "Yeah, that's unfortunate, but I mean, what can we do about child separations, or refugees, or drug prices, or school shootings anyway?" That's someone else's bubble.

So I profess my truest belief, at my core, is not to exacerbate or tolerate injustice ever again. While these problems are not our problems or issues—yet—God forbid, we cannot be antithetical of their impact upon us all. I haven't taken in any Syrians as of yet, or protested a drug company, or driven frantically to the high school to see if my kid is alive. So I could easily cop a bullshit-laden opinion of "Oh, how horrible," but an it-really-doesn't-affect-me attitude. But you do see, as a caring human, that some unnecessary shit is going down in this world and people are hurting, right? And so, at a minimum, let's not exacerbate things from the bleachers, safely within our bubbles. Let's not let our ego govern right and wrong. Let's forget about looking good, or how we avoid looking bad. Let's not just tolerate the intolerable.

The hardest thing about enlightenment is that hypocrisy hates confrontation. Or maybe it is more about our un-learning. Yes, I realize my own hypocrisy—my back-

seat-driving, coaching-from-the-bleachers, observer-only, not-donating-or-participating position from which I preach. Shame on me. Yet, I know I can confront mine. I can re-think things I thought I knew. I know I can be a better human. I know I can influence humanity in the smallest of ways, every day. Hoping that what I do, fighting the intolerable, makes a difference. A difference because I pay taxes, because I vote, because I object to things that are wrong and I say something, because I know my kids hear what I say and see my actions, because I know I could change someone's hate to love, or bad thoughts to good thoughts, or let them know that I understand, that I care. That I have been there and there is a way out.

So, Tim, my brother, I believe I know you. I believe you don't kill haplessly for pleasure. I believe you work hard. I believe you have enjoyed luck, fortune, and white privilege. You have had lean times, bad times, and good times. I believe no one has prevented you from doing what you really wanted to do. Ever. I believe you love and care. I believe you would stand up to bullies. You saved my ass on a few occasions too. I believe you see and know right and wrong. I believe you would die to save another. I think you want fairness, and to be treated fairly, and for others to be treated fairly. I know you help others. Love others. I don't think you hate. I think you are smart. You don't steal, manipulate others, or plot malfeasance. You pay your taxes and do your part. You are not afflicted with illness, and you really don't suffer in any substantial way, shape, or form.

Furthermore, you are modestly modest, well-mannered, self-deprecating, generous, gregarious, quietly intelligent, considerate of other people's feelings, and generally well informed, or at least should be well informed. You are expressive, fun, outgoing, honest, loyal, involved, and a great teammate, a great father. Your actions and ways of being are contagious, and people love being around you. You coach, you give, you influence. What you coach, give, and influence lasts. You don't teach cheating, racism, isolation, or bombastic intolerance to others. You spread your time, your heart, your fortunate knowledge, your love, and your essence to others. You are a top-quality human being giving to others so they can be top-quality human beings! You are amazing. You are all these things and much, much more.

I know this. And I know this because I know you.

So please do not be shocked to know the shock I feel about your political vitriol of late, as it counters and conflicts with whom I thought and believed you to be. And let me be clear: I can understand wanting a businessman in office, surrounded by experts at the highest level, all working together. That was appealing to me, although I voted differently. And granted, both candidates lacked abounding characteristics deserving of our worthiness or that of any human's political leadership. But that's all water under the bridge now.

However, the "let's-see-how-this-thing-goes experiment" has without argument turned out to be a shit-show. I could list five hundred things this president is, like he is racist—categorically racist, without concern or even denying the claims of his overt, ignorant racism. But as if that should not be damning enough of a disqualification, he merely does not embody what a decent human should embody, much less a person who is our president. He is not qualified. He lies, badly. He's a social disaster. And any high-brained human can rise above political rhetoric not to see things as being wrong, but moreover, and more importantly, as not being right!

Therefore, my brotherly hope is that this note will help communicate just a fraction of how I feel. My want is that it will help you understand what I meant when I said that my litmus test is "if a person is nice to you, but not nice to the waiter, they are not a nice person." That's just basic human decency. There are good humans, and not so good humans—and they group into tribes.

I want to believe that WE are pretty good humans. In the pursuit of that belief, I am perplexed by the mind-numbing political tribalism, but, so be it . . . this joker got elected, and I have to deal with it.

You and I know that if this president could articulate a smooth, coherent, and consistent message of empathy, logic, fact, and science, he would be lauded and beloved worldwide. Even one sentence, you know, the kind of smooth talking it takes to get a smart girl to go out with you. This is the guy who **can't** *do that. Instead, he buys hookers. He's that creepy guy. He's not the guy we need as president. 99% of the world knows it. 70% of America knows it. And you know it. And I know you know it.*

And if I am wrong about that . . . then everything I just wrote about knowing you was wrong.

So ask yourself this, when was the last time you were shocked to learn something? I mean really changed-your-world shocked. For me, this shock, it occurs almost daily. It first began on election night, but that lasted about a week or so. Then it got worse seeing how others vacated their scruples and bent their principles and their beliefs to be in line with his beliefs. And knowing that my brother, this amazing human, who is so deeply rooted in my life's development, my literal DNA, my daily life, almost suddenly, and tragically . . . how he fell victim to the spell of a lesser human . . . is shocking to me.

Look, our relationship does a couple of things: First, it provides the foundation to have this conversation. And second, it is so deeply founded in love, and trust, and

155

family, and history, and brotherhood—all at the highest level. And it will outlast this current political shit-show.

So to turn away from having blistering arguments about real issues is silly. Not talking about it? Well, that is not us. We can't hide our head in the sand. We can't take our marbles and go. Not over this, and not over the fifty years we have had, or the fifty years to come. This fuck-stick will pass. And I will most certainly bust your balls for eternity in loving, brotherly jest. So man up, Trumper!

See things through my lens. And help me see things through your lens. Break it down to your core, human beliefs. In the end, neither of us will be right about the politics. But at the core level, the level by which I know you, and you know me, we will be right as rain.

Tim, what I do know is this:
I believe I know the authentic and real you. You are one of the good guys.
I know you long to be with family, and not so far from your roots.
I know this life is short and we should work on being closer, not farther.
I know one day we will.

Wish you were here, with all my brotherly love! Shine On You Crazy Diamond!

—Phil

* * *

Postscript

This letter was belabored with extreme love and consternation and took me seven days to write. It took me all that time to get the words and the message just how they needed to be, with a clear expression of the main point: "I know you. I love you. We disagree. Possibility." I had to get every word right. I didn't. But I did for me. And I sullied my nerves enough to seal the envelope and drop it in the mailbox. It took another three or four days to travel through the mail and be received by my brother. Knowing my brother, it probably took a few days to read. I don't know for sure. My point is this:

My letter features a fully self-expressed, uninterrupted, and thoughtful one-sided conversation that was VITAL for me to have. I hated our two-way phone conversations prior. Arguing, not listening. This does not mean I won and he was wrong. It just means I resorted to a medium or tactic that allowed me to be FULLY expressed. Facebook was not the answer. Nor was Twitter. Human to human, they are not. A heart-felt, long letter featuring one-way communication technology, saying everything I wanted to say, in the way I wanted to say it. Uninterrupted. Unabridged. Stamped, addressed, mailed, was human to human.

Long ago, we used to write letters all the time, back when we licked stamps. We don't do either much anymore. Faster, shorter, immediate communication does have its benefits. But you would be mistaken to believe that the old ways did not work well. Sometimes, believe it or not, actually work.

In the days of waiting for my brother's letter to reach him, I would daydream about him going to his mailbox and seeing a letter from me. A fat nine-pager—stuffed, stamped, and hand-addressed. I dreamt of him opening his mailbox and being all like, "What the hell . . . ?" Then seeing that it was a real, full-on letter—from me! Then stopping and looking ahead through the nine pages to see if it had any pictures or cash stuffed inside. *"Nope, a full-on reader, damn!"* Sighing as he goes back to the front page and starts over. Then stopping again, thinking that he may need to park this letter till later, until he can focus on it. Pour a drink. Then read. I don't know how that all went, but ten days passed before he finally called, and we talked about my letter. We talked about everything, including the experience of getting a letter. I didn't change his mind about politics, nor did he change mine. What changed was the conversation. It was reset with precise calculation, where what we used to think was us talking (but wasn't) got upgraded to "two loving people of differing opinions able to have real conversations again . . . even about politics."

I have say-so in the matters of my life. I chose my words, I chose my brother over all.

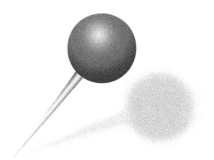

Align Words
With Thoughts,
and Thoughts
Will Win All.

Down With the Sickness

There is an old and solemn oath in the medical profession, I think it is long forgotten, that says: "Before you heal someone, ask them if they are willing to give up the things that made them sick." And there's another oath for medical practitioners, called the Hippocratic oath, that says "do no harm."

Oaths are, in theory, good things—but they're JUST words. And in fact, did you know, not all medical practitioners even use the oath swearing-in anymore? It's weird . . . but true. Many can't or won't, as it adds liability and even a literal challenge, that saying "do no harm" disables you from touching a patient, because you may hurt them and HARM them even in an exam. Much less for a needed surgery. *APPARENTLY* . . . cutting open a person harms them . . . quite literally. Even though the odds-on, greater good is being served.

I am not entirely sure how I feel about all that. You know, it's just words . . . and an oath. A swearing obligation, a declaration of agreed principles. You know . . . all those silly time-honored things that a judge does on a stack of Bibles. Our president. Our cops, lawyers, and politicians. Our priests. Hell, I think my insurance agent had to pledge an oath. I did once. I had to swear to tell the whole truth and nothing but the truth, so help me God . . . I thought it was cool, and then in a way I thought it was entirely unnecessary because I felt—I believed, of course—that telling the truth is easy if, you know, you don't lie. So I really had no conflict with the whole swearing-to-God thing. And for most oaths, you know . . . serving and protecting is a badge of honor, upholding the laws of our country and protecting our Constitution for enemies foreign and abroad . . . is COOL . . . and easy. So YES . . . DOING NO HARM should be a piece of cake.

Oh, and then there's wedding vows . . . lest we forget! I did those TWICE . . .

They're just words. Right? What is the harm?

So let me ask THIS: Is it the words that hurt? Or is it the person that hurts us? Or is it the broken promise of words . . . the violation of the intent and/or contracting of the words, as an agreement . . . that pisses us off? Is it the lie. The cover-up. Or is it the pivot and false narrative that knocks the wind out of us.

Does this bother you? Does it hurt you? Or us? Are you sick with it, as I am?

If you are like me, and your answer is yes . . . and you are sick with it . . . Then I have one more question: Are you willing to give up the things that made you sick?

Do you think words matter? Can you back it up? Some of us can, and some of us cannot, because we are too out of alignment with our word. Some of us just sling words and talk shit with unscrupulous abandon. Then, others conveniently judge and cast the stones. Some even mount passive-aggressive counterattacks at any do-gooder who counters their ideals, then demands higher standards for "OTHERS." Some do all these and more.

But that's not you, right? That'd be . . . well, hypocritical. We are enlightened, right?

If you are like me, and feel words matter . . . then pursue the accountability and the honor held by our oaths and our vows . . . and demand that others do, too. Yes . . . RESIST! PERSIST! and . . . INSIST!

THISday

But too many times, there are cracks in our suits of honor . . . we are, after all, not infallible. We all have crossed the hypocrisy line . . . just some farther than others. To say otherwise is a lie . . . unless Jesus is listening today. What's up, Jesus! But the honor is: If we fail, and falter with our words, our commitments, and our vows, we can acknowledge and expose our shortcomings and vulnerabilities—and give it up, clean it up, and . . . not cover up and conceal. Our words and our shortcomings are forgivable. Jesus did say that. And I believe him . . . and honor it. But I really didn't need the endorsement of Jesus to know that honoring your word is, well, honorable. And right. And if our words are in conflict with our actions, or our vows, or our oaths or our promises . . . and that is what is making me sick . . . then YES . . . I am ready to give it up . . . because lies, and broken promises, and sour words poison us all . . . And YOU know THIS.

Emma, THISdog I Know

For seven years, Emma has been at or near my feet. In the days that I have penned these words, she has nudged me, interrupted me, alerted me hundreds of times. She has needs. She needs me. For a pat on the head. Water. A walk. A treat. She's terribly spoiled. Or is it just me?

Either way, I now listen to her. She nudges me, and I say, "Just a minute." Then in a minute or two, she nudges again. And so, I go. In going, I find that I did need to take a break, just for a few moments. We get to the backyard, and I see that I need to skim the pool, pick up poop. Put the rake up. I notice the wind, the sun. It's beautiful. I say a little "thank you" to the universe and God. I clean up just for a few minutes while Emma chases a bird, chews her bone, acts like a dog. She takes another dump where I just cleaned. I wave at a neighbor. He returns a drill he borrowed. He says, "Let's have dinner sometime. Drink some tequila." I say, "Okay," again. We plan it for two-to-three weeks from now. He tells his wife. His wife texts my wife. My wife says to me, "Did you agree to a dinner?" I say, "Yes, in a week or two." Something about tequila? Of course, I said yes . . . duh. So two weeks go by, my neighbor says he's looking forward to tomorrow night. I say, "Oh, yeah." (I mostly forgot.) We go, and we meet up with other couples that we did not know, and we end up having some real and enjoyable conversation without the BS niceties or shallowness of inauthentic speak. A week or so later, one of the couples comes over with the neighbors for a visit. We sit in my clean backyard, with no poop. Drink some tequila. They meet Emma, and they love her instantly. And as I look at Emma and she at me, I would like to think that she knows all of THIS is because of her.

But I know she doesn't think like that. Why? Because she's a freaking dog! She just needed to poop. She just needed to scratch and roll in the grass. She just wanted my company, and she's neurotic and loves me and loves just BEING together with humans, and when she nudged me, and I said YES, instead of no, and I took the moments required to satisfy HER needs instead of mine—I found that I was WAY better for taking that time, because I got to pick up the rake, and the poop, say hi to a neighbor, and I made my wife a little happier because I cleaned the backyard just a little, and she praised me, and we got to go out to a fun dinner and make some new friends. THIS is what can happen; THIS is what you can have when you pull your head out of your ass! When you try. And when you listen even though you might not understand. And THIS happens when you quit saying "no" all the time and start THINKING and SAYING things a little differently, listening more carefully, and showing up more frequently. LITTLE THINGS HAPPEN that are WAY different and WAY better than you just sitting at your desk thinking you are too busy to be bothered by a dog.

Yes, I hope you get to know Emma!

Lobo, THISdog We'd Known

In the early '70s, my dad sold his farm and moved us to the city. From the Midwest to the Southwest for a change of life. In the city life, so much was different, like chores. Chores were completed in minutes, not hours. We didn't have to change our shoes to do them. And while my dad took an agricultural job at the university, the elements of command, control, and containment for his kids was changing, too. That change of life hit my dad squarely when my sister brought home a puppy and asked if we could keep it. You know, the old, can-we-have-one-animal-now-since-we-no-longer-have-hundreds-of-animals sales pitch. It worked! My dad had lost control.

Lobo was our new family member, and she smashed all the rules. All of them. And she transformed my dad. "Animals do not sleep in the house." Lobo did. And she slept in the bed. Don't get me wrong—he was still a farmer at his core. This once-quiet, simple, and hardworking man who suddenly started telling stories of how smart and talented Lobo was. He was prideful, joyful, and playful. He would spend hours after work watching her and playing fetch with her.

My older brothers and sisters were glib with his transformation. Maybe even shocked how he was now not only active and engaged with a DOG, but also active and engaged in the activities of my brother and me, the youngest of his six kids.

For me, my dad was at every football game I played in, from Pop Warner through college. He walked, then drove me to school, then worked side by side with me to teach me how to fix my own car. He hugged me and said "I love you" to me several times a day. No restriction, no curfews. All privileges that were not given in ample doses to my brothers and sisters when they were at home. Again, I am the youngest of six kids. My oldest sister is seventeen years older. And while we were raised by the same man, it was done so by two distinctly different dads in part because of Lobo. She changed his thoughts. His words. His parenting. His life and my life, too. My dad changed. We change. We can change. We can be changed.

Of Kids and Puppies

My dad was born a farmer in 1928 and raised as such, knowing that all animals had a purpose on a farm. Dogs and cats were needed on a farm. But they were not pets. Through this life experience, my dad's thoughts were that animals were to be commanded, controlled, and contained. Then cooked.

Animals were fenced, roped, branded, inoculated, clipped, herded, broken into submission, then sent off to slaughter at our bidding. For a farmer, it's not an "unwoke" insensitivity; that's just how farm life is. And for farmers, what was true then, for the most part, is still true today.

Technology and innovation has changed much for the farmer of today. But the basics remain—seed, nurture, harvest. Parenting strikes a near semblance to that of the farmer. Seed, nurture, and harvest. Commanded, controlled, and contained.

It is called conformity.

Bailey, THISdog I Knew

I met Bailey at a mall pet store in El Paso, Texas. We were immediately smitten with one another. My "want" for a dog in my life was a distant thought; however, I soon found excuses to go the mall on a weekly basis or more to check on Bailey. She, like all puppies, was just adorable. A little rottweiler, only weeks old. Each trip, I found a reason to visit her and each week I would notice that the "rotation" of available pups would change, apparently as the puppies were sold and replaced by new puppies. Each week, something new—except for the rottie. Every week, I would greet and pet all the puppies, but I was increasingly loving on Bailey. And she, on me.

During each trip to the pet store, all the puppies would do their cute puppy things. But when Bailey saw me, her eyes would light up like none of the others. Although I felt that I wasn't really in a position to take on a dog, I asked the store manager if there were any interested parties for her. The manager shook her head. "People are just afraid of rottweilers, I guess," she said.

In the following weeks I would go to the mall—admittedly for the sole purpose of seeing if Bailey was still there, not just to shop—and I was continually dumbfounded that no one had snatched up this beautiful puppy and taken her home. By now, this little puppy hardly fit in her kennel. "Any offers for her?" I asked.

"No," said the manager.

"Can I make one?" I said.

She was priced at $600! Of which was at least $600 more than I could afford. The manager told me they do not negotiate, especially on high-value, American Kennel Club dogs. But I shared my concern that this was nearing, if not already, cruelty for this pup, and said, "I would like to make an offer, and I would like it if you would call the store owner for approval. If so, I will take her now."

Ten minutes and one hundred dollars later, Bailey and I left the pet store as happy as two could be. A young man with his man-dog, and a new chapter in life for us both.

Bailey and I bonded so deeply over the next few years. It was a crazy, deep love full of affection. Daily talks, walks, and play. Long and loving stares at one another and symbiotic understandings. She had a perfectly charming demeanor and became well trained. There was a deep trust and confidence in her. She was stoic and perceptive. I guess it went both ways. She was a gentle giant, like me. Scary-looking to others, like me. And she possessed the innate ability to tear somebody a new asshole, like me. Two peas in a pod.

Have We Not Evolved?

In those few years, we two peas then became three peas, then four and five peas in a pod as I married and had children. Bailey and I had new people in our lives. New homes and new things to protect. Bailey did her job, as a steadfast and loving family member, like me. She never quivered and was consistent in her love, companionship, loyalty, and protection. She never changed.

I did.

Marriage. Work. Money. Kids and all of my "musts" had mounted in my life, and I succumbed to them all. Poorly. I was an unwoke decision maker and I somehow adopted a "slave to logic" thought system, if you can call it that, whereby I sought advice and input by others. The advice my dad had warned me about.

"You need this, do that, plan for this, buy that, your plate is full, sacrifice, commit, be decisive." All well-intended suggestions, no doubt. But these words and influences befallen upon a young and aspirational mind can be dynamite. Dynamite, as in the explosive. I felt I was an up-and-comer in life, and I thought all this "good" advice would lead to a better one. I mean, look at our influencers: bankers, corporations, bosses, neighbors. TV shows and fashion magazines all defining how our life should be, how it could be.

My then life was swirling and surging up, down, to and fro. My finances sucked, which is an entirely subjective opinion. I am sure my outward appearances—my clothes, my cars, my neighborhood and home—all looked like life on a solid foundation. But I was a mess, at every level. And when my three-month-old son became ill with a life-threatening lung infection, I snapped. With my self-imposed life-volume of noise now turned up to eleven, I said the unthinkable: "Bailey has got to go."

It could be argued that it wasn't a snap decision. It's just that I had made such shitty decisions along my path, and I had "accepted" such things as time and money, the influences, the noise and chaos, as the top end and the bottom end of my priorities. I somehow believed Bailey to be my chaos. And chaos had to get out of my life. I, judge and jury, planted correlation between my dog and my son's illness and sentenced her away. I packed, crated, and flew Bailey to my sister's ranch, eight hundred miles away, so she could live out her days. Bailey was maybe seven or eight. My cold and stoic self said "bye" to Bailey, and I went back work.

Work harder, move again. More bad influences, energies, and a divorce. In a way, I was glad Bailey missed all that. But that wouldn't have broken her heart. Only I could do that.

One day, my mother called to check in on things with me, and she casually mentioned how my sister was doing. Then I asked or referenced something about Bailey, and my mom effortlessly spouted out some words that I could not unhear. Words that were undoubtedly mistakenly said. She said, "Well, nothing will ever replace our Bailey." Stunned, then I slowly said, "Wait, what?"

My mom just froze on the phone, then stumbled, "Well . . . since Bailey . . . died. You knew . . . right? It was now . . . so long ago," she said.

"What? What happened? When?" I said as I choked down tears. My mom told me

171

that Bailey had died within a few months of getting sent to my sister. She thought my sister or someone else had told me. Bailey had taken ill, quit eating, and gone lame with colic, according to my sister's veterinarian.

I was crushed.

Still cold and emotionless, my domineering ego reminded me that sometimes we have to make tough decisions.

My whole world, at one time, had been just my friends and me in new beginnings—new starts that many twentysomethings have and experience. Then my entire world got better with Bailey. It got better when I married. And better when I had kids. And Bailey went through it all, like the loving champ she was. Bailey's world was great. Nothing but pure love. PURE. LOVE. What an asshole I was! I once loved Bailey so much, and she loved me. What the hell happened to me?

We have a zillion things in our life we love and cherish. Zillions. Bailey just had one—me.

Why, oh fucking why, do we do what we do?!

Not just with dogs. Or cats. Why do we go from managing (mostly) well in early life to a midlife crisis? It's not money issues, or job issues, or marriage issues, or kid issues, is it? Surely, I wasn't a revolutionary, a pioneer, or the first person to have a job, a spouse, some kids, and not all the money, right? What monster had I become?

Look, growing into adulthood, taking on jobs and kids, is normal-as-shit pressures that hundreds, thousands of generations of people have taken on throughout the history of being human. And still, have we not evolved?

Unchecked, we evade or succumb to normal pressures and to the noise. We quit talking, we quit listening, practicing, or honing our communicative skill sets. We get stuck. And we open ourselves to anything, and anyone's, advice. Advice that can be invasive and crippling.

I died a little this day.

Get the
right words,
get the
right cure.

Of Honor

Honor is a lens we all DO NOT have. Honor is earned.

To be honorable, we must learn honor. To learn honor, we must pursue understanding of our words.

"Honor your words."

"Honor thy Father."

"Honor this discount coupon."

Each pays honor to honoring some agreement of words, their meanings, and the promise that you will hold those words, and the people that use them, to their word.

To be honored and receive honors is a perspective bequeathed or bestowed upon others in recognition of a commitment or a delivery of a promise completed. The perspective lenses of honor only come as we learn to honor our own words. In other words . . . you get it when you "get it." When you stand behind your word, deliver upon your word, keep your word . . . you have honor, or know honor. And then you can see and seek with honor.

The perspective of honor is an honor. With it, you can see the good in others and in yourself.

We honor rules, and that red means stop and green means go. We honor the goodness in good men and women in the world, honor and respect their perspectives, and honor their wishes. We can honor honesty, and science and history and culture, our environment, and our neighbor. We can honor our needs. our wants. People. The game. Our strengths, thoughts, worries, ideals, job, passions, gratitude, commitment, ego.

We love honor. We all can have it, when you have it.

There's THIS Lady Who's Sure

Mom, FORGIVE me, for I had forsaken you. I am sure you know that because I sense that I am not the only person alive that must admonish our guilt. Perhaps it is the procession of life. Perhaps you experienced a version of this, too, I do not know, and perhaps I don't need to know anything other than what I am now learning, which is that I was borne by you, and I now experience being born and reborn every day. It's a fantastic gift you gave me.

I am not a religious person, just historically curious, and so I began to look into more about the Virgin Mary (because honestly, I had not thought that prayer to her was a part of what we need in life), but the more I pursued, the more I began to understand that her story was the bedrock for all of humanity and part of the commandment to "honor thy mother and father." Then, of course, it makes me think of you and the seeds of honor that I have had, and will hold for you eternally. I am fortunate that I kept digging, and while it didn't take long, I feel that I have now found the wellspring to water those seeds that you planted so long ago. As my ever-honored mother and as a cornerstone in my life, I found this prayer and thought I would share it with you.

THE THREE HAIL MARY NOVENA
ONE—In honor of Our Lady's Power—

Oh, Immaculate Mary, Virgin most powerful, I beseech thee, through that immense power which thou hast received from the Eternal Father, obtain for me purity of heart, strength to overcome all the enemies of my soul, and the special favor I implore in my present necessity. Mother most pure! Forsake me not, despise not my prayer, graciously hear me for God's glory, thy honor, and the welfare of my soul.

TWO—In honor of Our Lady's Wisdom—

Oh Virgin Mary, my Mother, through that ineffable wisdom bestowed upon thee by the Incarnate Word of God, I humbly beseech thee, obtain for me meekness and humility of heart, a perfect knowledge of the Divine Will, and strength to accomplish it always. Oh Mary, Seat of Wisdom; as a tender Mother lead me in the path of Christian virtue and perfection; enlighten and enable me to do what is most pleasing to thy beloved Son, and obtain my petition.

THREE—In honor of Our Lady's Mercy—

Oh, Mother of Mercy, Mother of penitent sinners, I stand before thee sinful and sorrowful, beseeching thee through the immense Love given to thee by the Holy Spirit for us poor sinners, obtain for me true and perfect contrition for my sins, which I hate and detest with all my heart, because I love God. Mother most merciful, help me in my present necessity. Turn, then those eyes of mercy toward us, oh clement, oh loving, oh sweet Virgin Mary!

Hail Mary, Full of Grace, The Lord is with thee. Blessed art thou among women, and blessed is the fruit of thy womb, Jesus. Holy Mary, Mother of God, pray for us sinners now, and at the hour of death. Amen.

This message is beautiful. When I discovered the prayer, it rang clear to my heart because of you. It reminds me of how I value you in my life. And I hope you enjoy seeing it too. I wanted you to know how I feel. How I hope. I pray. I work. I love. I support. And how I know I am supported and loved by family, friends, and God, without religion, yet with heaps of faith.

Most importantly, I wanted to say that I love you, and thank you for being a strong mom, a loving mom, a supporting mom, and even for being a tad-crazy mom, with all the Godlike traits that people should want in their lives. I am blessed. I will be eternally grateful for you.

When I talk with Hannah, Greyson, and Isaak, and I am reminded that, first, I was once in their shoes, struggling as a poor college kid full of life's ambitions, friends, new experiences, and all that occupies a twenty-year-old's life. And second, I am now made aware of what parents do to support our kids. We just do the best we can. We counsel, we give, we support with money and time, we sacrifice—and somehow, by the grace of God, we make it another day. Then those days add up and add up fast!

I am happy for so many things about my family. And I am learning about the ebbs and flows of life as it unfolds before me. A procession of struggles, countless distractions, decisions, ups and downs. They seemingly endless. Mom, I want you to know of my struggles. I know now, that as a parent, I would want to know the struggles of my children. I have resigned from the falsehood of covering or masking truths to appear other than I am as a means of saving you undue duress or causing concern. But even as I write this, I become awakened and sure you know THIS already.

May many blessings greet you with this letter, and all my love!

—Your most favorite child! ;-)

We Can Get What We Want,
Or We Can Just Get Old

Oh, how we forget our mothers. In a busy life, we forsake so many things, often believing that others will understand that we are busy. "That we are important." That we will have free time soon and all will be right in the world. Our mothers, well, that's just one example. We do this with our spouses, our friends, our kids, our parents, our neighbors, our allies, our countrymen. We do this because we are addicted to BUSY. Busy rules us in such a conniving way, laying waste to our "human" connectedness for the sake of money, or position, or some other accolade. It twists our priorities and bends our light, making us believe that we can excuse what's important, for expediency to a much freer "someday," where you will get to have all the warm and loving and special moments with all your loved ones, with all your time and riches to spend on them, too. It's a pipe dream.

Look, while we are not all born equal, we are all born of mothers. They gift us life. Mothers reveal our capabilities of LOVE, COMPASSION, and EMPATHY as our innate gifts. Those gifts, those feelings, which most humans receive, are our superpowers that shine though our UNDERSTANDING of this gift.

What changes us? What derails us from the promise and understanding of love, compassion, and empathy that our mothers give us, to that of judgment, of right and wrong, of hate and greed? Could it be our words? Could it be our words and what they are made to mean? If that is true, then actions are indeed stronger than words. Here and now, love and compassion are needed and felt through the rendering of care and necessity of provisions, which are a roof, a hug, warmth, love, food—which almost all humans need and desire. What changes us from using our innate gifts of love, compassion, and empathy to hatred, racism, and greed? Words and meaning change the game. The fundamentals of right and wrong are almost all word-based teachings. As are hatred, racism, and greed. It is taught to us and we choose to believe the meanings.

Let's communicate that we are NOT busy. Ever. And let's honor thy mother, for we all have that commonality. Let's honor thy partner, thy brother, and sister. Our neighbor, our co-worker. Let us talk slower. Walk slower. Be complete. Replace small talk with personal talk. Your type A personality is not a badge of honor. I should know. I spent years mowing over others in conversation and being untouchable, unknowable to loved ones. It does not make you more interesting. It just conveys that you are really alone, aside from the company your ego provides. That same ego that confirms that you're right, you're busy, and "that's just how I am." It's a complex. It's psychological. It's debilitating for all sorts of relationships. Look, we chase so many falsities, and the only truth we will find is that we have just gotten old.

I recognize that I am that guy, and in turn, my pursuit is also that my ego doesn't own me. My ego serves me. It is in this way, THISday, that I can change my relatedness to others with a fuller expression of human connectedness, that I can show love, give compassion, and share empathy. I cannot describe my love, compassion, or empathy. No words can be scripted to upstage action.

Real words, real listening, and real acts of connectedness speak volumes to others. You want different outcomes? Different words, different listening, different vulnerabilities, different ideas, different outcomes. Slow down in a fast world and you will stand out. You will savor more. Save more. Live more. Enliven more. Honor more. Guilt less.

Not guiltless, just less guilt.

To hell with your ego! Your ego is the asshole. You are not.

You are no more
the Victim as you
are the Powerless.

Retrospective Perspective

For some, the matters of perspectives will forever be a game of salesmanship. And if my career in marketing has taught me anything, it is that people won't buy anything that they don't believe will solve their problems or serve their self-interests of being richer, faster, or thinner. In marketing, we mostly present a common problem and magically show you the solution that leads you through a funnel to buy what we are selling. It takes some evidence or authoritative confidence that one, we know something you don't, and two, we have that solution already figured out. We add some seductive imagery, or language, and maybe a before-and-after photo depicting dramatic and instant gratification or intimidation . . . from fat to skinny, sad to happy, or poor to rich. It's pretty basic, because so are consumers. Consumers are human, and humans have basic security needs, and insecurity triggers.

Over Time, In Time, Outta Time

It is complex, and the process can take a long time. Along our path, we can get stuck in our perspectives. Even with a preponderance of evidence and authoritative before-and-after arguments for new thoughts and ways, people may still choose the old perspective or paradigm. (Think "flat-earthers," climate deniers, and conspiracy theorists.) But in time, our perspectives can change significantly. Just in my life, I once believed Columbus discovered the Americas and that the US won the Vietnam War. My perspective changed as new information, new discoveries, evidence, and fact were written for discussion and deliberation. I was a Republican once; not anymore. I changed after a preponderance of information and fact challenged my old beliefs. I once even believed in the tooth fairy and "until death do we part." I once thought mullets were cool and BlackBerrys ruled and no one drummed better than Neil Peart (okay, that's pretty much settled science!). I thought Bailey was living a better life and government was honest, along with cops and justice and priests. Those perspectives have shifted in me, and may continue to shift. Why? Because I am not stuck or still in life's current paradigms. I am not afraid of trying on new lenses.

Having perspective is a strength, whereas limited perspectives are, well . . . limiting. An openness to new perspective is a servant of growth, expansion, and possibility. It can add layers of faith to the faithful and debunk the falsehoods of previously "sold goods" like trickle-down economics. Perspective can keep us in the know and in the now. Perspective can unstick us and assist us and protect us from being pushed down or passed by. By the simple fact that perspectives generate questions, and thoughts and conversations create space for all of us to fit in and participate in creating our life and our days with venerable purpose. While we may not like the view from new heights and new vantage points, and we may fall back to old paradigms, that is okay. But Knowing, Understanding, and Respecting are just the start. And denying all other perspectives will be your end.

Do we really want to limit or not welcome another's perspective? Not if you are only focused on Mickeys. New lenses aren't new. They are just new to you because you hadn't changed your lens. With new lenses you can see, seek, and experience new, better, and different aspects and potentials of life. New, better, and different thoughts. Questions. Ideas. Beliefs. You can find better words. Create different moments, better days. Better weeks, months, years . . . and lives. In this hunt, recall the lesser-used lenses of PROVIDENCE, POSSIBILITY, HOPE, KARMA, GOOD FORTUNE, and PRAYER. Lest ye forget their evil-twin lenses of DOUBT, SUSPICION, DESPAIR, JUSTIFICATION, GUILT, JUDGMENT, and MARTYR.

Knowing perspective is a privilege we give ourselves and their lenses are not burdensome; have as many as you would like! And remember, we are no more the victim as we are the powerless. You are not a victim, and you need not be, if you do not allow yourself to be. You are not powerless, unless you say, think, and believe yourself to be. Unleash yourself. Unleash your most powerful weapon: your words. Think something. Say something. Be Something. Do Something. Have Something. Change something. Change your lens, change your perspective. Participate. Change the world. What are your lenses?

186

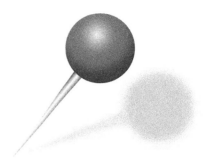

You have talked
yourself into this...
You can talk yourself
through this...

Rock Bottoms and Mountaintops

Here is the story of the story no one cares about. It is one of dozens, if not hundreds of stories that need told. Why? Because it is my story. I had to write it. It was easy to write. I knew every word, every detail, because I rehearsed it in my head and wrote every word. It consumed me. It became me. Here it is and you are sure to despise it.

On November 9, 2016, things just changed for the worst. It is my "now" point of singularity. I voted for Hillary, but she wasn't my first choice. The fact that American voters had just elected an idiot was mortifying to me, and certainly to the majority of voters . . . as in the MAJORITY! But I sucked it up, somewhat, and I went about work and life with the essence of okay-ness and a makeshift cloak of righteousness. And blame is better to give than to receive.

In March of 2017, I traveled abroad on a planned vacation, meeting and apologizing to Europeans along the way as they discovered I was American. In return, I received hugs and consoling, many wishing us luck, strength, and words like "hang in there; we love Americans—you guys will figure this out." I began to prepare our customers for what I believed to be the new political environment. But after that, business got even worse.

In May of 2017, my biggest customer left me after seven years with only thirty days' notice. Consumer confidence plummeted. It was a plague. A deluge. It was like a dream turned nightmare, but it unfolded into a daily nightmare. That kind of nightmare that for some reason I couldn't wake up from. I thought, "I'll just wait it out." That was far from my worst mistake, but let's just say that that dream continually worsened.

For more than a year, the income that had slowed, then trickled had stopped. We cut back, but not fast enough. And I watched my month of pay become my year of pay. I know you're saying, "Oh, you're a 1 percent guy, right?" Hardly. And fuck you—don't judge me. In all my life, it wasn't until the last few years that I had really good years of income. Finally, as I approached fifty with three kids in college, I could give real support. But now back to zero? What the fuck was that? A cruel joke? When do I wake up? When do I get the lesson? Have I failed the test?

"Be thankful for what you have." "Give Gratitude?" "Stay Positive?"

Am I Job? What did I do to you God? FUCK! I am FUCKING TRYING!

I've made it into the new year, credit maxed out. Food, mortgage, car, and insurance all in jeopardy. I have not figured it out. I have not had a break from this nightmare. Should I be thankful? #BLESSED? Nope, I am not there just yet. It's tough to fake being blessed. Not tougher than burying my brother's son, which didn't give me any sense of blessedness. Cutting all reasonable things like healthcare, healthy food, clothing, TV, restaurants, travel, gas, car repair, home repair, parties, family trips—all those things are gone. That shit costs money. I didn't anticipate new legal costs. Not sure how that's going to get paid. But that's mostly wants and just a few needs. What I really need is to wake up from this dream, this nightmare. You know, that mindfuck dream where I have no extra money and I'm still scraping coins for the homeless beggar. I do it for Karma. And I think, "Is it a double trap? Why did I not give more? More often? Why now? Is this a guilty dual-track Karma issue? Or will I wake from the dream and see things get better, only to realize that I was in a dream inside a dream? What's next? A dead dog? Cancer? A twisted ankle? Shingles?" I have no hope for thoughts and prayers any longer. Don't console me. Don't tell me to "hang in there." I'm still in the game, but I need a fucking rebound and a few three-pointers or I will be out of the game. Then I will meet you on some street corner with a sign. Asking you for money. Why is it so quiet? No one calls except the bill collector. He knows I'm quite literally barely keeping the lights on. Oh, I am thankful for that. Do I praise you, Jesus? I would, but it doesn't yield anything but hurtful emotions because I am not suffering—the only people suffering are those whom I support. No, I won't give up on God, but I don't understand anything or any lesson and this praying nonsense seems a tad overzealous for a guy who just needs a break. What is worship? They say good things happen to bad people and bad things happen to good people. I can't explain it in any meaningful way or context other than I know I am not the only asshole who's going through this. God, I hate comparisons. They are seldom fair or accurate; they are false equivalencies, and they steal my precious joy and hope I once had. God, I will continue to walk with you, and I will take this beatdown. I will own it, and eat it one-bite-at-a-time. Who-moved-my-cheese? Who cares, the cheese made me fat and slow. In my life, I have had it good, and I have had it great, and I have had it bad. I'm just not sure how badly I need or want it anymore. What is my purpose with you God? I want to be reborn, but fuck it, I am here now. So what is it? Fight or flee. I have talked myself into this. I can talk myself through this. God, I am ready! I am ready for my life to change! So, it's fight, motherfuckers! I'm doubling down—you ain't seen nothing yet!

Sometimes writing out your truthful complaints and life rants is cathartic. When I felt I had hit my rock bottom, I did just that. And I will do it again. Shout it OUT! The above is exactly how I felt, and so I wrote it. Not with the intent to ever share it, but instead to shame the "story" and to shame myself for thinking it. This was my story that I made up and told myself over and over, like it was God's truth. But the truth was, the story I was making up was killing me. I was suffering. The story might not even make sense. I just had to write out what I was feeling. I had to get it out of me. No time for grammar. Just purge. Yell. Grunt. But write the real words, thoughts and feelings. Read it out loud. Read it again. See the poetry and the insanity of what we tell ourselves. Expunge your self-pity. Free your ugly parts. Get it all out. Then, like an ancient sacrificial act or ritual, light the page on fire and watch it go up in smoke and ashes. I don't really know why I do this. I am sure I read it somewhere. Fuck it. It's pseudo-symbolic, but it works somehow.

These are my words. My meanings. My acceptances. I had to write them. I had to own them. Forgive them. And ask God for forgiveness, for it was not his punishments, they were mine. They were the words I said, and the thoughts that I had that created the feelings and the stories I believed to be true. I had to send them away in order to begin a new story, and create a new path.

Look, my rock bottom and your rock bottom are probably two way-different places. My mountaintop may be your doom, but let's keep that in perspective, shall we, at our next pity party. And at our next mountaintop celebration, let us also remember our former Sherpa-selves.

What's your story? Are up you ready to give it up?

There's No One Like You

My marketing beliefs and my core beliefs fit who I believe I am. Who, presently, do I believe myself to be? I am different; I take a different approach—a different risk. I believe the lower the risk, the greater the conformity. Here, the real risk in marketing is not being real with other people. In marketing, my customers know I am different. Some clients avoid hiring me for that very same reason. Look, being real has some real setbacks. And I have to be real right now. I have lost business opportunities for this very reason . . . being honest and real. I wanted some of that business. And I have been tempted to bend my beliefs, just to earn some business. But, in almost all instances, I have been thankful for that outcome and not bending principles in order to win. Is the answer to "why?" obvious? In business and in everyday life, it is increasingly desirable to only work with elevated thinkers and people who value our truest selves. In doing so, we grow. I do not fault those in business, and in life, who desire or ask others to bend. Being flexible is an enviable asset to possess, and an inescapable rabbit hole to get lost within.

Making Me Like You Is a Risky Business

One objective, or principle belief, I have in marketing is: "Make me like you." My clients chuckle when I tell them that, but it's pretty much a rule. Being likable is pretty easy to do. Many advertisers come close to hitting that objective. Most car dealers miss it by a country mile.

MANY CAR DEALERS WANT TO TALK TO THEIR MOTHERS, WIVES, AND DAUGHTERS LIKE THEY WERE HARD OF HEARING AND MOSTLY INFERIOR OR DUMB. I THINK THAT IS DUMB. FYI.

I—and most people—are repulsed by those ads.

So why all the bad advertising? Well, the challenge is, when marketing to real, everyday people, is getting over the noise. Companies sometimes run crappy ads because . . . wait for it . . . THEY WORK! At least I think so. Why else would they keep running them?

But here is a perfect example of what festers in us. We put up with a little bullshit from everywhere. Not just in advertising, but in our jobs. In our friends. In our relationships. We get caught up in it. It's called mediocrity. But unlike the ads we dislike, we allow mediocrity in all aspects of our life. We relate to mediocrity as "good enough" or "normal levels." It's the kind of mediocrity that can and will define you. The kind of mediocrity that may be more precisely defined, in my opinion, as "acceptance of ignorance." It shows up in other aspects of our life like, is this it? Like, this is what I get? I work hard all my life, and this is what I get? Okay. I accept. I'll accept the condescending speak. I'll accept my pay. I'll accept minimum effort and consideration of my intellect. And crappy commercials, too.

When you hear or see a bad commercial, you have options. Click the channel, call the advertiser and complain, or keep watching it over and over. You can accept the way people talk to you, or not. You have a choice and can speak up or shut up.

Choose courageousness or thoughtfulness. Choose to try or not try. Change may not happen, but it is available only if people HEAR you and LISTEN to you when you decide to do something in order to change something. At the same time, if you say nothing, are you not accepting mediocrity? So we must figure out how we can be real. You can figure out any new assembly of words to have a conversation with your boss. Your kids, your parents, your anybody, for any situation. Can you be real about your needs? Your wants? Your ideas? Your thoughts? Your feelings? Or will you accept things how they are; that your voice won't matter?

Make me like your answer.

It Is Up to You

You get to choose your words. You don't get to choose the outcome of your words. You can make better use of your words to give you a better shot at changing the conversation so as to change the feeling, change the opportunity, change the level of mediocracy.

Like I said, being real can be risky. I can SPEAK LIKE A BAD CAR DEALER. I can also say nothing. I can be real with my words. All are risky forms of speech. Speak up or shut up? Risky business indeed.

This isn't just about getting your way all of a sudden, and the car dealership may not change its ads to please you. Why? Because it is not about you. This is about changing the course of your life with the meaning and application of your words that are put forth into the world to enact potential outcomes, different from what exist now. It's not about their words. It's about your words. Trying better ways to assemble your thoughts and feelings into more powerful tools and have your words mean more in this noisy life is gutsy. And this is a no-rules way of just being real to yourself, for the chance to impact new and different outcomes is transformational for your human soul. We could say that most of us have a mediocre life, but I choose to describe my life with better words, and by sharing those words with the world in ways that can crack the mediocrity crisis. By doing so, it causes a shift in me, my related happiness, and possibly the outcome of our conversations, our choices, our opportunities, our way of living—it's just words. Find them. Know them. Say them.

The world now, today, THISday, is the culmination of every word ever spoken. The culmination of every word ever received, ever heard, ever listened to and understood. Or misunderstood.

Wordsmithing is the height of the game. It's how you play the game. How you win it. Wordsmithing is the game itself. Our words, our letters, our lyrics; our pillow talk and careless whispers; our texts, emails, and tweets—their collective effectiveness is a matter of nothing other than our ability to create meaning and understanding. And to do so in a manner of timed and succinct arrangement. Doing so requires the want of mastery in the art of wordsmithing—to tell a story, convey a message, make memorable and concise communication of uniquely assembled words—but the wanting, and the having, of the "goodliest words" may seem daunting or to not suit who you believe you are.

Wordsmithing, whether it suits you or not, can be the most rewarding of all endeavors, and a key to all endeavors. Wordsmithing changes minds, hearts, and the world. It's not more words. Really, why use two words when one will do? It's not louder words, either. It's just well-thought-out words, organized, precise, and articulated; delivered, received, and understood. The art and the science of meaningful communication.

Wordsmithing can be courageous. Bold and direct, with a risk of insult or retaliation—perhaps. Wordsmithing gambles on clarity vs. rudeness, tactlessness, and/or ignorance. It exposes ambiguity or cultivates it. The words we say to others, the words we say to ourselves, can be satiating or inert. Choose. Choose from an ultimate selection, endless variety, a pallet of shades and boldness, words for every occasion, or choose not. Either way, it's still a choice.

Wordsmithing is a journey, never to be completed. We may have the words one day and forget them the next. Even when we forget them, they can come back to us, magically, miraculously. Or not.

If wordsmithing is the game, can you play it better? Can you start today? Can you think before you speak? You can and you should. Because words, like a hammer, can drive a nail or shatter stone. Words are our most powerful tool in THISday's arsenal. They are our antecedents to every thought and feeling. Choose.

Allow the journey
to be its own story.

Trusted Voices

My in-laws don't speak English, but oh, how they adore me; and I adore them! My father-in-law, *mi suegro*, spends hours talking in the worst broken English and Spanish you will ever hear. He sings every Beatles song I play—horribly. And I sing "Te Lo Pido Por Favor" even worse. Tequila? Sure, there's tequila involved. But the headache comes from the unscrambling of the meanings we try to share, not the excessive tequila drinking. Our conversations are not simple. They are complex, and our language differences vast. One thing that is not complex: the understanding between us—that I love him, and he loves me. We work through our language difference to HAVE a conversation. We both wish it were better. But it is what we have now, and we don't avoid our awkward and belabored chats. What we have is perfect. We don't lament much about what we don't have. We don't quit. And we understand it as such, as would two children from different countries only need to play together to communicate and "be" together . . . that is what we have. We HAVE that because we wanted it. We needed it, and so we create it. From this creation, he truly knows the man that married his beloved daughter. I know he knows it, not just from the words we manage to get right with one another, but from our nonverbal conversations that send clear messages. We have completed a circle of communication. It's more than the cultural hugs, kisses, and endearing "*gritos*" (our greetings and proclamations); it is known through our patience and willingness to play regardless of the outcome. We get what we get, every time we talk. If it is a wink, a nod, a laugh, or a broken word or sentence, we are playing, and we get communication. And in this gringo's THISday . . . I understand that he loves me even though he has not spoken those words.

I have graduated this spirit and crafted a living by playing well with others regardless of our challenges. Irrespective of our differences. I have done so, by trying, sharing, and coaching what others said I couldn't do. In doing so, I have not only bridged a gap and showed gringos the spoils of communicating to Latinos for business marketing, but I have also assisted in the investment of tens of millions of dollars of marketing investment into the US Latino marketing space. Today, my gringo car dealer cuts commercials I write, prepare, and translate into Spanish . . . wonderfully. He is adored and embraced by both English- and Spanish-speaking consumers. My gringo "language acquisition" client started with just $8,000 in 2011. And he made the Hispanic Top 20 list in 2017. My gringo tax client rules the Hispanic airwaves and is a Top 5 advertiser according to Nielsen rankings (2017).

For more than thirty years, I have thrived in the Hispanic culture for these reasons: I showed up. I listened. I tried desperately to understand. But most importantly, I tried. It has taken years. Patience. Ridicule. Relationship investment. It has taken gumption and failure. It has taken so many wrong words to get to the right words. It has taken relentless determination. And while I offer up this personal reveal, I want to say that it's NOT about me. It's about the process. About the pursuit of understanding, the investment of time and dedication. About caring and perseverance. To think you can roll into any situation with your type A, B, C, or D personality and come away with your expected outcome is silly talk. You have got to give and give and give with no expectation for immediate gratification. Life is not a gumball machine. It's more like a slot machine. Life is about investing in people, and a place where a word or two—shared, understood, clarified with heartfelt sincerity—will almost certainly pay a lifetime of dividends and break barriers. It is trust built over time.

My business is about trusted voices. To some, maybe just a few hundred people, I am a trusted voice—people who got to know me over time, and trust what I say. In fact, my go-to "snapshot" secret in marketing is the use of what is called "trusted voices." Three of my few hundred people who trust me are Eddie "Piolín" Sotelo, Dr. Cesar Lozano, and Alex "El Genio" Lucas. If you don't know them, that's okay. That's why God invented the Google Machine. But if you do, you know that these three iconic nationally syndicated radio hosts, these rock stars of Spanish media, have more than 15 million people who trust and follow them every day. That earned trust came from years of communicating from their hearts and their souls. Each talent found new and different ways to convey a message of honesty, sincerity, and compassion, along with fun and humor, to win the hearts of millions of people. When our paths crossed, we shared many poorly pronounced words and built a foundation for sustained business growth and friendship. No one is an overnight success. I wasn't. Piolín wasn't. Cesar Lozano and Alex Lucas weren't. Neither were any of my clients. However, our collective words and efforts have elevated us to where we are at this precise moment, which is at the top of our game.

Are you a trusted voice? You can be. *Sí, Se Puede!*

enlightenment:
May be more about
the Un-learning

Turn, Turn, Turn

You are entirely entitled to feeling shitty, tired, sad, fat, lonely, under-appreciated, un-loved, mad, upset, depressed, gleeful, cocky, arrogant, right, wrong, busy, stressed, important, superior, mean, stupid, et al.—anytime you want. These are common feel-ings. But being any one of these all the time sucks for you, and likely sucks for others. Inevitably, your BEING runs into someone else's BEING, and you either meld into one or start a nuclear reaction of epic proportions.

While you are entitled to these feelings, you are equally entitled to choose not to have these feelings. The truth is, you usually DO choose these feelings. We were created to reign over our emotional consciousness. Two people can respond dif-ferently to the same event, like a canceled flight. One rants and raves, yells at the airline personnel. The other takes a seat and waits for the next flight. Both voice/ego/critics are working fine. Neither response improves their respective positions and inconvenience.

The remedy for silencing the voice/ego/critic is setting an appointment. For exam-ple, let's say you are mad. You are mad because you just found out that your signifi-cant other had an affair with your best friend. Man, you are mad. Your NOT YOU voice/ego/critic is pumping out pure venom. Death, kill, stab, revenge, tears, guilt, remorse, hopelessness—whatever keeps you safe and right. Your NOT YOU voice is doing its job. But you have a job, too—an important one. You're a surgeon, a cop, a kindergarten teacher, and you got to be at work in an hour.

You see the issue yet?

If you are my surgeon or my cop or my teacher, I hope you are reading this.

Even though you did not choose to have your significant other cheat on you, and the timing sucks (I mean, is there ever a good time for anything bad?), you CAN choose to postpone your emotionality, your revenge, till, say, 5:00 p.m., right?

Say to yourself, YES I AM PISSED, but I got things to do, so I will have to be pissed off later. Set an appointment. It's that simple.

Attitude Platitudes

Let's deal with the critic issue first. The critic is the voice in your head that is NOT YOU. That NOT YOU critic IS needed. That voice does a lot of good for you. Primarily, it tries to keep you safe. For example, that voice often tells you what to wear, like "Hey, you need shoes or a coat." It also tells you when to "RUN!" because it's in emergency fight-or-flight mode. But that voice also stops you. Limits you. That voice berates you, shames you, and keeps you from trying things—again, primarily to keep you safe.

Keeping you safe is vital. But this voice works alongside your ego. That means this voice/ego/critic says things to you in your head like "Those pants make you look fat, and you eat so much, and I told you not to eat so much, now everyone will just hate you more if you wear those pants, even more than they do now, because you're fat. Put on something else and let's go eat." Yes, all that was said to keep you safe. Odd, but true.

For your NOT YOU voice, it's just doing what it is supposed to do. Therefore, it's true and working just fine, because it keeps you safe. Safe, because it is feeding the ego of being right. Your ego loves being right—and hates being wrong. Therefore, working in tandem, it's doing you a favor: keeping you safe and right. Right? Whether you are indeed fat or not, if the pants make you look fatter or not, which may be entirely empirical, is not the point, nor is it the job of the voice. The ego. The Critic.

THISday

It's deep.

My job is to have you understand THIS in a way that can quiet the critic, the voice, the ego for your betterment. We will never turn off the voice/ego/critic. We can't and do not need to; after all, we need it to keep us safe.

To quell the voice/ego/critic, we set appointments and permissions.

As a Matter of Factors

There are chemicals. Habits. Layers of the onion so thick with "storied feelings" masked as facts. Quite inexplicably, it's life. Yes, it happens. It's true. Maladies happen when you (your voice/ego/critic) add meaning to the events that occurred in real life. Perhaps your cat died. That is life happening. In life, there is death. Fact. "I am so depressed. Or life sucks," is the made-up life that happens after the fact.

But unless it is YOUR death, everything is just "an occurrence" that you get to hang your perspectives on. I am not being insensitive here. THISday is about you, not me. My THIS and your THIS are different, yet our THIS consists of exactly the same options. It's just a chosen perspective. And this is just mine.

Yes, we are all touched by the news of a school shooting. Our emotions grow from "Oh no . . . not again," to thoughts and prayers, to outrage!!! But it's different if you are the kid who got shot. It's different if you are the parent, friend, or loved one. It's different if you are a survivor.

Your silliness about wearing fat pants seems a tad shallow now. Your NOT YOU voice/ego/critic stops just for a moment, because something else occupied your mental agenda. Yes, AGENDA! Things on any agenda move and change every second, minute, or hour of the day. You set the agenda. You set every last thing, which means you can purposefully change it. It does not hold you hostage. You are not a victim. If you feel that you are a victim, try—try—to give yourself a break and reset the agenda.

I do not intend to minimize your feelings, suppress your feelings, or mask your feelings. Any feelings. You simply must bring to presence the fact that your feelings are things, subjective things, and those things can change, and you can change them. It is a matter of perspective. Choose wisely.

Feelings produce chemicals; that is a fact. And in fact, chemicals will change, too, once you govern your agenda. Okay, speaking of change, "Ready? Okay. Two bits, four bits, six bits, a dollar . . . all for me, stand up and holler!" I know this is a lousy example of a cheer. How it came into existence would be interesting to know. I do know it's a much better cheer than you usually give yourself—ever. Some people would say that their mom or dad, wife, husband, brother, sister, friend is their greatest cheerleader. That is a nice thought, touching to hear. But it is cliché.

Again, cheerleaders don't cheer for you. They cheer for themselves. It makes them feel good or worthy or supportive. Maybe hopeful. I am not knocking cheerleaders. My euphemism is, however: Those of us who provide hope, motivation, support, positive vibrations, high fives, or thoughts and prayers, we are simply on the sideline—NOT in the game. My dad wanted my team to win so bad, yet he knew nothing of our game plan or how to execute it. He cheered when things went well. He cheered for us to "get 'em next time" when things didn't. I love that he did that. I love doing that, too.

What THIS points out is that we must find our inner cheerleader. And no, your boss or coach, or life coach, or mentor can't pull this off. They don't qualify, either. Sorry.

The truth is, our inner cheerleader is ALSO our NOT YOU voice/ego/critic. Yeah, the YOU that is definitely NOT YOU is the YOU cheerleader YOU need. Bummer, huh?

Before that NOT YOU voice/ego/critic tells you to jump, just know this: Your NOT

YOU voice/ego/critic is not only there to keep you safe and right; it is also there to help you win. It is there to help you figure out complex problems. Easy-peasy, right? It really is. But like anything, mastering it takes a bit of "doing" and "talking." Practice, too. And like anything, it doesn't guarantee outcomes. (I thought we covered that already!) But it does improve the odds in your favor tremendously.

Keep on Rolling

What are the easy things? Role playing and visualizing. Easy because you have heard of them. Refining them to work well for you takes practice. Repetition. Athletes do this well. In our minds, we conjure up the actions, the events, the minute details involved in our intended effect. The imagery, including all the senses—sight, sound, taste, touch, and smell—is all present. Rehearsing, seeing, experiencing the event playing out successfully, over and over again in our heads. Our imaginative selves can create nearly anything in our minds—so much so that our minds can hardly distinguish between the visualizations and reality. It's a fantastic tool.

Yet interestingly situated right next to your whole "visualization" show is your NOT YOU inner-voice/ego/critic watching the entire thing. This is the time you want to set the appointment for him or her to come back after the event. Once the action is over. THIS is very important to know.

You see, it's hard to un-see things you've already seen either in reality or in your mind. If doubt, failure, or nervousness conjures negative images for you, then you have a real battle to deal with. While feeling uncertain and nervous is normal and good, allowing those feelings to manifest as visualizations of failure, demise, or error can improve your chances of failure. Fear, anxiety, and worry do play a role in our success as a species. Sensing fear creates chemicals in our bodies that ready our muscles to respond. The chemicals cause our brains to think critically about our options to fight or flee. Anxiety is akin to fear. It is a fabrication of fear but produced and experienced without any real threat. Just the thought of danger can create anxiety. Many of us avoid scary movies because we don't like to experience fear. Many of us want anxious feelings to go away because they can be traumatizing and limiting.

Experiencing anxiety can be quite healthy, however, as it often provokes idea-producing thoughts. If we understand our processes and our anxieties, and work with them, we can change the outcome, change our experience, or produce the next big thing for the world.

Envision a meeting or a presentation. Envision it going the way it should. Every detail. You can do it. If you can't picture it, then call for the spirits and the gods and the universe to send you the best words for that conference, argument, paper, book, or talk with your spouse or kids. Call them to magically come to you, on command, right when you need them, and they might show up. Look, you know all the words. Envision your test going well. Envision getting a B instead of a C. You can just as quickly see it as you can BE it.

You can even envision the unknowable. An unknowable event or endeavor, such as death or a trip to Mars, can be envisioned without it being a scary thing. Our vision is limitless.

What is limiting is the voice/ego/critic. Ask him or her to come back in an hour. Or in a day. Don't let them have an opinion when you haven't asked them for one.

Lastly, there's one other trick to master, which I mentioned earlier: exposing the ego. The voice/ego/critic hates being exposed. When exposed, it suddenly will do anything to deny its exposure or even its existence.

THISday

"Oh, your ego is disgusting!" someone says. "You're just saying that so you feel good about yourself." Or "You're just in denial." What's the immediate response? "NO! I'm not! It's not!" the voice/ego/critic fires back. Yeah, the voice/ego/critic fights back when exposed. Why? It's caught off guard. It's embarrassed. And what's its job? To keep you safe and right.

The trick in dealing with the voice/ego/critic is to talk to him or her regularly. It's healthy. It's not the same as talking to yourself. Because the NOT YOU voice/ego/critic is not you. The NOT YOU voice/ego/critic is like an acquaintance you keep running into here and there. You can acknowledge them just by saying, "Hey, I know you are there." You can go a bit further and say, "I know you are there, and that's cool and all. It's just that I need to get some things done for the next hour or so and want to ask if it is okay if we talk tomorrow, or after the weekend? Is that cool?"

Literally. You can say, "Hey, I am not happy that you are here right now. Can you please go and come back later?" Or whatever you want. Merely acknowledging him or her in a YOU to NOT YOU conversation in your head, or out loud, exposes the NOT YOU's presence and minimizes its grip on the moment. Its grip on you. When you do this, the outcomes change. You change. The world changes in an instant. Try not to outthink this or overthink this "trial." If you are, it's the voice/ego/critic in you right now saying whatever it is saying. This is the fight. Your fight. If that fight is happening right now, the goal of the exercise is just to try it. Then try it again. Train to be YOUR cheerleader. You really, really need one. No one else can do THIS but you.

NOT YOU, NOT YOU, go away. Please come back another day!
NOT YOU, NOT YOU, go away. Please come back another day!

That's a new cheer you can cheer. No one who cheers for you could ever make a difference in your life more than you could by just cheering for yourself.

Martin Luther King Jr. said, "Darkness cannot drive out darkness; only light can to that. Hate cannot drive out hate; only love can do that." Dr. King was not cheering us on or giving us a pep talk. He was giving us the keys to the kingdom. Shining light on our darkness. When YOU exposes the NOT YOU, the NOT YOU will retreat. This life and THISday is what we make of it. Who's making the call? Who's deciding? YOU or NOT YOU? THIS life will not get better when other things get better. THIS life gets better when you get better.

Woke words are
worth more than a
thousand pictures.

Completed Days

My dad was alive 31,213 days.

However, I am not sure exactly how many days he *lived*. That would be at best subjective, at worst judgmental.

I hope I have that many days which hold for me the opportunity of *living*, but I feel that I am running out of tries. I have already passed 18,000. I sometimes think that if I am given just one more try, only one more day, I would promise to sit in my backyard, look at the trees, pet Emma, chat with a few folks, write some notes, have a few tequilas, and call it a day.

What would you do?

From one perspective, days are just days. They are quite ordinary. There have been billions and billions of them. And billions more to come. Each one of them is almost nearly the same as the last. Same as the next. The same length. The same average temperature. Half of them dark, half of them well lit. Pretty common, cosmically.

We, on the other hand, get very few of them. I had a friend who only got 6,000 of them. Some people got all of theirs before we got ours. It's all random—you kind of get what you get.

We all spend our days differently. Some of our days go fast. Some slow. But again, that's subjective, right? It is how we experience our days that matters to us,

THISday

for some reason, and then again, a day is still just a day, cosmically.

If given just one more try at a day, your last day on earth, why should you spend it differently from any other day? Would you have a blowout? Or would you cry all day, sad that it was your last? Would you lament your regrets? Ponder your legacy? Bemoan your bucket list? Would you apologize to everyone, forgive everyone, hug everyone? Would you pray? Confess? Organize your will? Would you even tell anybody that it was your last day? Or would you let everyone know it was your last day? Would you pick a final meal? Drink your good wine? Would you find your final spot—a picture-perfect, last-vision-on-earth spot? Would you make your bed? Would you tell everybody what to do after you're gone, you know, so that you can control their future? Would you try to do a little of all of this?

Are Best Days Ordinary or Extraordinary?

It's funny to think about your last day through these varied lenses. It's quite morbid, too. None of this sounds soothing or peaceful. So let's hope that you have more than one day—otherwise, you're likely to be really busy for about twenty-four hours. Then what? Who knows? But whether it's one more day or 30,000, the exact number of your days left is not typically yours to decide. What you do with your days is.

"Live each day like it's your last" is an unfortunate cliché. It's a cliché because it's a worn-out phrase, and it's unfortunate because it's bad advice. While well-meaning intentions are behind it, we too often seek to patch the tough things in life with these way overused expressions.

Please finish these clichés for me:
"When the going gets tough . . ."
"If at first, you don't succeed . . ."

I'll stop. There are a zillion clichés. One-liners, short ways of making a whimsical, cheeky point. Zingers, we can even call them. We like them. We say them. We text them, alter them, post them, and misuse them. I have probably written several zingers thus far that people could post in adorable fonts over an image of a setting sun. I hope they help, just like I hope thoughts and prayers help.

But if we could speak our heartfelt intentions with thoughtful language, delicate precision, and careful timing, our message could have a greater impact. We could contribute to the collective of positive energy, solace, and support. Well-thought-out and well-timed words work. Woke words work.

Thoughts and prayers might help, and your prayers might be answered, but likely not. God, the divine, and the universe are most definitely not gumball machines.

Mourner: "I am sorry for your loss. My thoughts and prayers are with you."

You: "Thanks for saying that."

Mourner: "You're welcome. It's the least I could do."

Me: "You're damn right, it's the least you could do. The VERY least. You should have shut up, hugged them, and left."

Now, before you start saying prayers against me, I'm simply expressing that saying something that's already been said over and over again is, at best, only a Band-Aid on a too-gaping wound. Additionally, if the weak words and clichés you used could heal the grief or somehow return my nephew, who indeed just lived his last day, I am all in. Until then, it's WORDS—THOUGHTS—FEELINGS that make us, us.

Time in a Bottle

Why couldn't we live it like it was our best day? Like any other day. Did you forget to do some critical tasks, or say the right words during the days you had? Now you want to, again, cram it all in just in time before it's too late. Cramming for a test or cramming to meet a deadline is way different. Your test date, or your deadline, is likely known and disclosed far in advance. Your DEAD line isn't. Even if the doctor has given you six months to live, you didn't promptly get out your calendar and pencil it in, did you? "Tuesday, 9:15 a.m. Got It."

Look, I don't know what your "wound" is. I don't know anything about what you are going through. I am saying that it doesn't have to be how you are currently experiencing it. You are choosing the experience. A self-inflicted experience. You may be a victim of some horrible deed. Your experience is simply your manifestation and creation of just how big a wound you have that needs mending. Some wounds won't mend. Sometimes cancer wins, bullets find their mark, accidents happen, we get fired, divorced, embarrassed. Sometimes we lose, we are burdened, guilted, shamed. But most certainly, our days will expire. So people deal with their "wounds" differently.

Our understanding, our knowing of what we can change and what we can't is paramount. There is only what happens. THEN there is what we make it mean. Two things that will never be one. Your wound is just your wound. Nothing more. If not,

THISday

how is it then, when your wound heals, the story, or the anger, or the grief remains? How long will you tell that story? And why? Think of the time spent, or wasted, and the undue pain these stories have caused you and others. Where does it stop you, or limit you? Or others? The time spent on immovable stories from long-healed wounds is the time not spent on the things we can change. We can change the words of our stories, and we can stop the fabrication and the distribution of our untruths. Or not, and resign to the untrue facts. By choosing so, we can change our understanding of what happened, and we can then tend to what we want in THISday. By choosing not, your hopes will die. Pathetic and all too common.

Dodging Death

My dad never saw or felt the extraordinary, for all we knew. He showed very little joy, exuberance, or pursuit. He was a "someday" dad, you know, "someday when we hit the lottery," then we will live a little. He seemingly resigned from "trying a life" early in life and was ready to die for years. He was crazy. Crazy for his kids, but sadly, his mind succumbed to his worries and thoughts and his someday stories that never came to be.

My best attempt at understanding the crazy in us all, is, in a word, "completion." Having completion is a magical gift we can give ourselves. Being complete is a grace and a renouncement of envy. Striving for completion should be the goal. And you must be complete even if you don't reach the goal. You were in the game. You didn't choose the game, but if you lived a day, you were a part of it. How did you play out your days?

Pope John Paul II, on the other hand, confronted his story and forgave his would-be assassin. Crazy? Maybe. Maybe not.

Go for It!

Pope John Paul II was in the game for 22,275 days. Then he got shot. Four times. But it was not to be his last day. In fact, the Pope got exactly 31,000 days out of this game. True. From May 18, 1920, to April 2, 2005. But on May 13, 1981, he took four bullets from the gun of an assassin who wanted him out of the game. One bullet hit his finger, another hit his elbow, and two entered his abdomen. Somewhat miraculously, the Pope survived his attacker's assassination attempt, and his wounds healed rather quickly. Except for the wound to the Pope's soul. It became evident that Pope John Paul II had pressing, unfinished business with his attacker, even though justice had been served with a life-in-prison sentence awarded to the villain.

Against the wishes of Vatican leadership, the Pope wanted to meet his attacker face-to-face. The media went crazy with the drama. Even the attacker said no to the request. But the Pope pursued understanding. It wasn't that the Pope just wanted to meet his attacker; no, the Pope needed to meet his attacker—to forgive him. The Pope forged his way and met with his attacker anyway. Not just once, but several times. To this day, no one knows the full content of those meetings. What is known is that the Pope talked at length with the assassin on many occasions, blessed him, prayed for him, and forgave him and ultimately changed the story for both of them. Eventually, in 1983, the Pope freed the assassin from prison with a full pardon. Without getting all willy-nilly here, that's completion, at so many levels. Neither the Pope nor his attacker ever revealed an explanation. The act was personal and deep. And complete.

I would like to believe that my dad was complete in his later years. Most of his life he longed to be a better provider. That was his only issue—his own shared issue—that I recall hearing him speak of. Even so, there is absolutely no evidence of him chasing an unfulfilled achievement; there was no grave, lingering wound, or sense of many re-grets. For the most part, he maintained a simple life and kept his words to a minimum.

As my father became more and more unstable as he aged, he, of course, knew that he was slipping mentally. It was dementia and something near Alzheimer's, we were later told. We were complete with how he was and how he was not, even though his path could have many different endings. He chose it.

My best guess is that completion, or the lack thereof, in one's life, or family, or workplace, or relationships, is likely an ever-present presupposition. Nah, I am just kidding! It's not. It's experienced and learned like all the other genuinely unimportant happenings in our lives. It is manufactured from the "what happened" to the "what we make it mean." It is a good lesson or a bad lesson that we choose to believe is the truth. Then we nurture it into our lives, into our years, months, weeks, days, and moments with impunity.

That's what my dad did.

Pope John Paul II did not.

Use the Force

Would you agree that a teacher who taught your kid that 2+2=5 taught your kid a bad lesson? Yes, most certainly, you would. What if a teacher or a parent scolded your kid for missing ten answers out of a hundred questions on a test? What lesson is taught in this example? A blatantly wrong one! When teaching doesn't truly teach, when the emphasis is on the score or the test, not the comprehension of the content, when that style of teaching locks your lesson into a behavior, potentially for life, that behavior can be passed down to others "because that's how I was taught." Or it can make you shut down. Or impedes your want and willingness, your drive to try, try again "because I hate criticism" and "I don't want to be wrong" for some unknown reason.

This is particularly daunting knowledge. It's tough to know and tough to recognize what stops us in life. And how it, or we, stop others.

If you think I am going to give you the answer because I have it all figured out, I can't . . . I don't know the answer. But what I suspect, and what I do know is only what I have experienced—it is way more feeling than fact—but my words, as a corporate trainer, made racehorses out of plow horses. Moved C-performance players to A-performance players. My words have burst bubbles, they have broken hearts, and they have inspired complete strangers. In toll, I can choose to be accountable to my words, my stories, and how they reverberate into the world. You can, too. When I recognize where my words have faltered, not benefited the world and have made a mess, I can clean them up. You can, too, while you still have days left.

My dad demonstrated deep love. Pope John Paul II showed exemplary forgiveness. Not all of us can pull off those two "life's little gems" well, if at all. My dad demonstrated a deep love for his family every day. And I want to believe that Pope John Paul II showed exemplary forgiveness every day. These are the lessons and stories to be recounted.

I choose to continuously TRY to make sure my words have real sentiment and a real chance for relevance in the hope that they are not just heard, but that they are understood. I am not sure if they ever are. But I quit saying "I told you so" an eternity ago. That phrase bears no fruit—not for you nor for anyone else. I am sure my kid DID NOT clean his room more than 0.0000001% of the million times I told him to. But it wasn't the end of the world. I was complete with how things were. I didn't make my son wrong or ground him for not cleaning his room. I kept asking, in a thousand different ways. Whether he did it or not had no bearing on my life's outcome. Or his. Nor should it matter.

He will have his challenges in his own life. The cleaning of one's room is not one that matters. Demanding someone to listen, follow orders, and respect parents or elders is taught many, many ways. By force is certainly one way to do so. But that may have many limiting consequences. With force comes resistance. That's science—and the overarching theme of *Star Wars*!

Being complete is knowing that you aren't always right, or the best. It is just being complete. It's just a grace you give yourself. There are no absolute "musts" in THIS life. There are only a few days, and you get to choose what you put into them. Then

225

THISday

they are gone. You cannot put one more thing into yesterday. But you can put many things into THISday that can make a better next day—if you get one. So I don't rely on thoughts and prayers, or clichés, or multistep affirmation programs. They have their place. Just don't let them replace human-to-human interactions.

good words,
good thoughts,
good feelings,
good friends,
good family,
good life.

Yes, "Probability"

Life is made up of a lot of little things. Good things, so cheer up.

Your life is made up of a lot of little things going in your favor. That one ovum that met your one spermatozoon that one magical night was just one of those little things that worked in your favor. That favor was the chance favor of millions upon millions of favorable things that became you today. And the you today—yes, you—you are so incredibly lucky. In fact, up until the day you were born, statistically you were essentially the equivalent of all of the winning lotto numbers, ever, rolled up into one. Then squared.

Since your birth, your luck has perhaps stalled somewhat. While this very day is still a reward for your good fortune, you can oft relate to it quite the contrary:

- I should have been born a woman or a man
- My parents sucked
- Why wasn't I born into wealth?
- I couldn't get into Ivy league schools
- My spouse left me
- My job sucks
- I lost my job

- My dog died
- I was picked last—again
- My life sucks
- You wouldn't understand
- It's real

Well, c'mon. Unlucky was being born into the mid-fourteenth century during the bubonic plague. Why are you crying?

The substantive truth is that you are here now, and it may seem that life's luck has recently slowed for you. Especially in comparison to the extraordinary luck it took for you to be here at all. Or are you comparing your luck against others? What they have and what you have not? Your station or position in life? Where they are, and you are not? Who has the power, and who does not?

In your defense, you must consider all that is around you, all the people and all things that are just as lucky to be here, too. What you are noting is that some people seemingly have been having a tad bit of added luck. That's probable and a valid argument. That's also both temporary and controllable.

So is it just about luck, and you are just a victim of bad luck? Do you think you have any say in the matter? While truly bad luck happens and misfortune spares no one, we can improve our odds. Hundreds of bad things can and will happen to us, and we can persevere. Or we can succumb to our misfortunes, give in, give up, comply, lash out, ridicule, not participate, be a martyr, and seek solace with like-minded, poor-luck souls.

Choose.

OUCH, Quit It!

Let's change the lens and look at it another way: Death by a thousand paper cuts is still death. But it is a stupid death. If you haven't figured out by around paper cut number 900 or so that this isn't going well for you, well . . . that's on you.

If the loss of blood and the painful little things that somehow happen to you, and seemingly only you, add up to something more serious, well . . . maybe you should have tried some other tactic to stop, slow, or prevent it. Stopping it. Slowing it. Preventing it. All would have changed your luck. Death by paper cuts could have been cured by now. Man, they would name buildings and streets after you! Wouldn't that make it a great life?

Look, life is just life. Days are just days. What we do with our days, and our lives, matters. We have SAY-so in our days and, thusly, in our lives. If the words that are said or the events that occur cause us little painful cuts, we can stop them. We can slow them down. We can prevent them entirely. Yes, I understand; in this metaphor, not all cuts are just paper cuts. Some are deeper and more painful. However, if the cut has not killed you, you still have a say in the matter of your life. You can change your luck. You can change your days. You can change your life. You can because you have SAY in the matter. The things that happen and the things that are said are all manageable. It's all in what meaning you assign to those occurrences. This is similarly correlated to our lessons in basic fifth-grade science when we learn that energy is matter—quite literally in the physical and scientific sense. Therefore, if words and thoughts have meaning, then meaning has substance and weight, or mass or form, and therefore is measurable. Now that it is measurable, we can apply some fancy long division onto the problem, and we can reduce the stuff in the middle, and we can come to a "SAY/MATTER" or a "SAY over MATTER" as your least common denominators.

In elementary school, I was horrible at math, but that, my friends, is simple "reductionism."

This was a purposeful transition to one of my shit-life stories. Mrs. Bright was my fifth-grade teacher. My story went like this: In the fifth grade, I once missed a math instruction that covered long division, and was lost in math class evermore. Throughout middle school and high school, I didn't just struggle at math; I failed. I squeaked by to graduate high school, and in college, I was sure to steer clear of any math-oriented degrees. As luck would have it, my first job out of college included a smack-in-the-face induction of math. Business math. Estimates, percentages, commissions, margins, statistical tendencies, year-over-year analytics. Complex yet also pretty basic math. My induction was sink or swim. I chose to swim. I got over my math issue pretty quickly. I could do the math. But I loved my sad, shitty story about how I missed a day of math way back in the fifth grade and it led me to forever being lost in math classes for the rest of my education. It allowed me to underachieve in math and overachieve in sympathy. My math deficits were survivable. But I had to change the meaning of my story . . . and it took me ten years to do so.

The things we tell ourselves aren't absolute truths. Neither are the things other people tell us. And for that matter, the things we tell others can be pretty messed up, too.

THISday

Over the years, I've found better ways to say things. I had to. I was now responsible for teaching others how to get by a little better in this world, in their jobs.

Please note, I said I found better ways. Not best ways. Not THE way. And indeed, I found worse ways. But in all my trials and tests, some basic math elements came back to me: PROBABILITIES.

I surmised that changing things was a matter of PROBABILITY. Yes, probability.

If every morning I stubbed my toe on the bed and it caused me pain and anger every day, which began my every day with a pre-set emotion of being pissed off, and then I was grumpy with my wife, kids, and dog . . . so much so that they would avoid me, not talk to me, divorce me, not come to my funeral . . . well, I could change all that. Easily. Probably just by moving my bed. That is probability. That is, the probability of improving your day by mitigating obstacles, hazards, potential pitfalls, and known upsets is a quality investment and statistically viable. It's just smart.

Don't stub your moments, days, or years on stupid words. Move them.

Why Don't We Make Known Upsets Disappear?

I've found that, in general, making people happy feels good. I feel good; they feel good. Add to that, when I feel good, and they feel good, better things happen. I've even tested that theory and found that, in general, making people unhappy feels bad. I feel bad; they feel bad. When that happens, better things do not happen. It's amazing what we can do when we feel good.

Can you make other people feel good? Can you make yourself feel good? Can you make people feel bad? Can you make yourself feel bad? Of course you can—with just words. And others can do it to you. You know this.

"But I am not a good communicator. I am not good with words. I am shy. I am just this way. I hate confrontation. I love confrontation." Whatever it is, whatever you say, you're right. So what? You are right, and your conversations fail. You are self-defeated, but you are right.

You didn't end up here by any other fact than the words you said, heard, and believed. Your future has the same promise. In ten years or ten minutes, wherever you are will be determined by those facts. Therefore, don't look to change others, or set expectations for any changes, unless you change what you say, what you hear, and what you choose to believe. The attitude, demeanor, or approvals of others matter not until you accept them as fact. If they are indeed a fact, then words are what determines or confirms them as such. Words are what will navigate your path and your future.

I have also found that I can't make everyone happy. Conversely, I've found some people make me unhappy. As this occurs in our lives, what discussions are needed for us to find our collective happiness elsewhere? Tough conversations. So we have them and move on to our next moment. And we start again.

Over time, I've found that the small things add up and become big. Small good things and small bad things equally add up. They don't add up just using addition; no, THIS was multiplication. With compounding interest.

I learned and practiced, then I taught my teams that probability math was much more favorable, our odds much improved, and our luck much deeper when we talked more clearly and listened more deeply. Statistically speaking, if we improve our behaviors, our rewards will grow. Our problems, our let-downs, our depressions were smaller. Our highs were higher—money, luck, love, fun, happiness—everything! THISday was better.

How It Came to THISday and the Fight of Your Life

Now, finally, the "secret" of THISday . . . really. When I speak and coach to groups and teams, I stress a few key points to unlocking the secrets of THISday.

You are in this game, and you are in a fight for your life, daily. Your yesterday may have been a tough round, but you survived. From nature, we know that the saplings that withstood the storm are now the oak trees. We know that the growing grass does not struggle to break through the hard ground. And we also know apple trees produce apples.

No other species on this planet aspires for "tomorrow" or for a "someday," except us.

So why the constant struggle for more or better or different? Why the suffering? Why the feeling of sacrifice, the sense of loss or confusion or misunderstanding?

The fight for your life *is* the story of life. The chapters may be good or not so good, but a book always ends. Those good and not-so-good chapters we get to write—every word. The end of the book, well, it will come.

In books of fiction, we can write all sorts of fantasy. We can create every character, the setting, backstory, and the ending. In our nonfictional life, we cannot add one more thing to yesterday, nor can we write for tomorrow. We cannot write anything but today, THISday—it is the only thing we can change.

THISday

Your yesterday is now fiction because how you tell that chapter is laden with layers of lies, half-truths, and subjective rhetoric. Your tomorrow is forever fictional, full of hopes, and someday wishful thoughts and prayers for something new and different. THISday is your only day for truth.

For me, how it came to THISday was by telling stories that hopefully reinvigorated something in you to do something new today. How it came to THISday was a process that took unbelievable courage for me to share. Not that I demonstrated superhuman powers. I just found my human power that we all have, and I used it. I shared my love and my words—with no attachment to outcome (because that is future, right?). Our human powers are under attack. They have been tamped down by the suggestion of conformity. "Wait your turn, stay in line, don't speak truth to power because you will lose." Fighting conformity is a struggle. But recognizing that you have been asked to play the game and follow its rules is a suppressive and unfortunate agreement that bullies, fosters timidity and can provide a source of disempowerment.

Theodore Roosevelt's most famous "Man In The Arena" quote stirs me every single time I read it. But THISday forces me to raise my hand and ask why are "those cold and timid souls" cold and timid souls?

It is not the critic who counts; not the man who points out how the strong man stumbles, or where the doer of deeds could have done them better. The credit belongs to the man who is actually in the arena, whose face is marred by dust and sweat and blood; who strives valiantly; who errs, who comes short again and again, because there is no effort without error and shortcoming; but who does actually strive to do the deeds; who knows great enthusiasms, the great devotions; who spends himself in a worthy cause; who at the best knows in the end the triumph of high achievement, and who at the worst, if he fails, at least fails while daring greatly, so that his place shall never be with those cold and timid souls who neither know victory nor defeat.

It is an amazing quote, of the highest inspiration to me. And at the same time I find conflict in that the vulnerable and the suppressed are shamed for knowing neither victory nor defeat. Timidity, or vulnerability, or venerability is neither a grouping of persons, nor a personality type, nor a sickness or condition; it is a symptom of action or inaction. Or perhaps it is a result of reaction.

Is the Cold and Timid soul encouraged to participate? Are they made welcome to participate? Or are they dismissed by gender, color, or physical attribute, or by education and ethnicity? Have we built a system, a game, a complex machine that produces the cold and the timid? Is the Loss of Power just a loss of power, or is it a loss or lack of capability?

237

THISday, I just raised my hand. Why? Because I have played in the arena. I have won. I have been beaten. I know how to overcome adversity. Yet, at times, I am among "those cold and timid." I question and doubt how will I keep picking myself up from the ground. I question why climb the mountain again, because at the top is just another valley. I question it all. Why? I question it all to find the answers. I question it all to understand. I question it all because I have a day to make, and I have things that I care for along my journey to enlightenment . . . and maybe I will meet my hypocrisies. Maybe I can make a difference, to myself or another. I question the perceived powers and find ways to the right path for a better moment, a better day. THISday, I can do something about it.

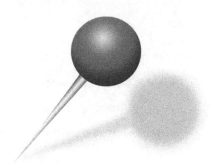

The journey does not require sacrifice or suffering. Neither do your stories.

It's Always 11:11

It's 11:11 again—of THIS I am sure. Fully, now, one half of my life has been aware that it was time to think, act, and do. Something. Anything.

Thinking is doing. Acting is doing, too. That is what 11:11, and all its iterations, are to me. For some reason—really, pick any belief or reason or theory—11:11 entered my life, and no one will ever know why. As much as I pursue the meaning, I will not know it. What I have come to find is this: It is not scary, it is not random coincidences, it has meaning and purpose. It comforts me, secures me, and makes me smile dozens of times each and every day. It centers me, quiets my ego, and splashes me awake each and every time I see it, and its iterations, as if they were a cosmic "nudge" from the nose of the divine universe. Just like Emma, whose interruptive needs are constant reminders that she needs me and I need her. And that, if I have awareness and presence of mind, I can "act" and "do" something, and be amazed by what this disruption of hers provides to my life, which is this: Our moments and experiences are meant to change us and to disrupt us. Our darkness is disrupted by light, and our light exposes anew all things for us to bring forth into our days. To wake each morning is to "awake" or to be "woke." It is to be enlightened; to be in the light.

When you pursue THISday, and shine the light on areas of your life that you have not yet fully understood or conquered, you too will find that they are not scary, they are not random coincidences, and they have meaning and purpose. For some reason—really, pick any belief or reason or theory, you entered this life and the light of THISday, and it should comfort you and warm you with security and contentment, each and every day. Allow it to center you and quiet your ego, and allow it to splash you awake each and every day, in all its iterations, as if it were a cosmic "nudge" from the nose of the universe.

The "learning" of how life should go has likely been told to you. You have likely been influenced by a marketer of life, who wrote into a script how to think, feel, and believe. What else did you think marketing was about? The marketers of life have told you time and again that you should buy into things that you didn't even know you wanted or needed when you woke up this morning; but you stubbed your toe, again, on some cosmic corner of the bed, and you are not sure just how to rearrange your world so as to not do that again.

That is 11:11. That is THISday. What it is to you, I pray you find when you shine your light on this life of yours.

Afterword

If the words that come out of our mouths are determined by what goes into our minds, then truly, what becomes of our days is determined by what we put into them. Garbage in, garbage out. Kind thoughts in, kind thoughts out. Hate in, hate out. Love in, love out.

I have so many things in me. I had to get THIS out of me, and into the world.

I hope you realized that I was on this journey with you, ever since page one. Every word, every sentence scrutinized . . . in some fear of retaliation. But I had to get it out, or in the words of Seth Godin, "hit the send button."

Who I am matters. I am Philip Gabbard, and I can say so. I want the world to know me, and I wanted you to know me ever since page one. But I feared. With each step forward, I experienced doubt, anxiety, and a sense of the need to retreat. In my weak moments, I would say that I was scared to death writing this to you. It was personal. But not anymore! For now I am free of my inhibiting demons who said "no one will care." I braved the corners of my mind, walked endless hours in my office, examined my relationships and my experiences to find words and stories that shared my innermost thoughts, and that may even help me rise above the noise; even if the noise is only in my head. Because every day we continue our pursuit of understanding, we find that we share so much in common. We share a love of humanity, of kids, of stories, of music, of old cars, and new experiences. We share the love of spirituality, of work and productivity and community, along with a touch of curiosity.

Throughout my life, I have been confronted with my humility. Was I told to be humble? Or was I born with it? I do not know which is true. But it comes up again as I think to write a few words "about the author." And they may prove to be the hardest words to write. I am not "nothing." I am humbly yours. That is what I am. I am humbly a son of a farmer and his wonderful wife of sixty-five years. And I am the humbled husband of the most beautiful and caring wife, Gabriela, whom I lovingly call "Mi Reina." My children are Hannah, Greyson, and Isaak, who continue to humble me as I think, "Wow, did I do that?" And of course, there is Emma . . . who is part golden retriever and part soul mate.

In my omnipresent self-discovery and journey through THISday, I have found a new cheer, and it is to be complete in all that I do. Yet to understand life's conflicts with our opportunity to be enlightened will unfortunately escape us all, but the pursuit *IS* the journey. What a journey it is, and may we never find the end of ours. Instead, let us take care of the journey, and let our experiences, our perspective, and the love we give to consume us and transform us to live THISmoment, THISday, THIStime, THISonetime, THISweek, THISmonth, THISyear, THISlife, THISchance, for the betterment of all things in creation.

Belong to the pursuit, and not to the tribe, and the enlightenment will be yours to find.

Thanks for reading THISday and may we THRIVE!

Final Acknowledgment

I would like to tell one last story about my editor Jack B. Rochester, and it is important that I do so. As I write these words, Jack is a man I have not yet met in person. But Jack is an angel of mine, without doubt.

When I submitted my manuscript of *THISday* for review by potential editors, Jack was not among them. I came to know Jack through a separate inquiry I was making for a different book proposal—perhaps my second book. Jack loved the ideas I had written and he remained in contact with me about them. Meanwhile, the editor I'd hired for *THISday*, went missing. Her whereabouts, and rationale for abandoning my fully paid project, were and still are (to this day) unknown. While I held much concern for her safety—and I have faith, or perhaps reason to believe, that she is indeed safe—I still needed to finish *THISday* and get it published.

On the day that I finally determined that I'd need to begin my search for a new editor, I received an email from Jack just checking in on how *THISday* was coming along. "JACK! The worst thing ever has happened," I said as I went into my tirade and guttural breakdown. Jack said, "Maybe this is a good thing." He went on to say how he loved my concepts in *THISday* and that he'd be happy to take over. "You're hired!" I said without a moment's hesitation. And with that, Jack got to work on *THISday*.

As many know, and as others can imagine, writers and editors are not always simpatico. Jack knows this more than anyone because as both an acclaimed author of numerous books and an editor of more than forty-seven years, he knows the book business. Jack is tough, gruff, and gritty. He is direct and honest. He is a deep thinker, and he is lovingly kind. And I only know this because of his words that he has shared with me during this editorial process.

Within sixty days or so, Jack had furiously endeavored to help make sense of all that I had written. As you now know, I write different, and Jack knew it, too. But Jack did not coach me to be someone else; he just feverishly worked to get me to write with the utmost clarity, granular honesty, and heart.

One evening, about halfway through Jack's second pass-through reading of my manuscript, he sent me a triumphant message via email. "I got it! I have figured it out!" he said. "It's Montaigne!" To which I responded: "All right! . . . Umm, who's Montaigne?"

I am still not sure (to this day) whether I am more humbled and honored by the compliment or amazed by the fact that Jack even knew who Montaigne was in the first place! Whether Jack's opinion of my writing is spot-on or way off, he worked to help me find my voice in a way that was just, and true to who I am. He did so with a sense and care that made me envious and hopeful for all humans and our ability for connectedness. Yep! Jack did his job. Then came the surprise, even after my final manuscript was done and my bills were paid, Jack said, "I would like to see *THISday* through to the end." He went on to say that my road ahead would be full of unruly twists and turns and that he'd like to work with me whether *THISday* sold one copy or thousands of copies. He said, "I feel I have made a friend in you. And in forty-seven years of publishing, I have not had the pleasure of working with a kinder and more caring author than you."

Come on! Who says that? And how does that even happen?

It happens because I shared some words that created some thoughts and fostered some feelings with a man that I have not yet met. Jack is an angel. Yes, he is an angel that I have prayed to know and to meet, and to have in my life. He guides me. He listens. And he restores hope in me.

May we all speak the words so well to have our angels present themselves in our lives.

Thank you, Jack B. Rochester, for being an angel in my life. I thank you THISday and shall thank you forever more.

The Making of THISday

THISday: Modern Essays of Enlightenment was born from the intention of enrolling others into a dream, a dream of sharing my words and stories with a wider audience. As I gathered my nerves to make such a bold request of friends and family, and of complete strangers, I was time and again stopped and stymied by my thoughts and feelings about asking anyone to support my dreams. "They are my dreams—why should anyone support them?" So I took to writing my words, and re-scripting my words, and speaking my words to see if I could get them right. And to see if I could convince myself of crowd-sourcing resources and finding support for *THISday*. Even after writing the best words I could find, I still needed to undergo the grueling task of recording them, then sharing them, which was emotionally torturous. "What would people think? What if I fail?" I then asked myself, "Why do I need any support at all?" And my answer: Because I want to get this dream fulfilled. I want to get *THISday* done right. I have a voice. I have changed lives. I have the know-how and ideas that can help others. I want my kids to know that despite all challenges, we can pursue our dreams . . . and it takes the right words to get the right thoughts.

So I said them aloud, recorded them . . . and hit send.

Thousands of people heard my words and listened to my request to fulfill a dream. Hundreds liked, shared, and followed my efforts. And eighty-eight people stepped forward with vested support to help underwrite *THISday*! I was rendered near speechless.

On the final day of my campaign, as the last contributions poured in, and as I saw that I was going to meet and exceed my goal, I cried. I cried because something had shifted in me. I had spoken up, and I had spoken out, and people responded. *THISday* would see the light of day, and it would be given every opportunity to help others to discover more from their days solely because a few people listened as this otherwise quiet man spoke.

I am and will be eternally grateful to those eighty-eight people. Many of which I acknowledge by name here. Others unnamed for privacy will, too, forever hold my gratitude.

248

Chris Reams	Karen Pearson	Russ DeVries
Justin Lowenfield	Simon Hernandez	Tim Gabbard
Miles Lowenfield	George Henman	Tom Rauchut
Luke Lowenfield	Kevin Childress	Audrey Barcenas-Burch
Ronald Lowenfield	Brian Hoffman	Hilary Warthan
Dirk Koetter	Rudy Acosta	Ben Van Horn
Amanda Ali	Heber Gandara	Patrick Hegarty
David Candelaria	Jacob Dayan	Joe Bell
Dave Burke	Matt Crofts	Charles Andrew Whatley
Carlos Moncada	Kurt Minko	Tom Humphries

Robert Lee

Andy Avila

Victor Reta

Sandra Bigelow

Terrie Todd

Jimmy Davis

Doug Morgan

Jennifer Hayes Temple

Anna Marie Fernandez

Deanna Ruiz

Richard M. Ruff

Rosibel Santiago

Lennie Rogers

Joseph Valdez

Cindy Stanley

Alexis Ferguson

Richard Wright

Laura Saldivar

Vicki Melvin

Candice Ingo

Chris Zarate

Anthony Caputo

Lisa Celaschi

Dan Dodson

Ed Krampf

Veronica Lowenberg

Matt Moore

Marina Lee

Karla Diaz

Gina Diaz

Kari Larson Dougherty

Kathrin Pettit

Brady Gilreath

John Jackson

Claudia Santana

Matt Gonzalez

David Edsall

Anthony Siracusa

Joe Fife

Howard Morgan

Andrew Blease

Ann Williams

Ray Larson

Shawna O'Briant

Drea Thomas

Kimberly Procci

Eduardo Cepeda

Hannah Gabbard

Isaak Thurber

Gabriela Castaneda

Joy Slusher

Lynell Walker

Neal Topf

Steve Haskins

William Gilpatrick

Mark S. McDonald Sr.

Christopher Roman

Traci Hickson-Romo

Greyson Gabbard

What to Do Next

think

listen

talk

read

write

question

pursue

share

smile

love

breathe

hydrate

pray

meditate

sing

be

thrive

For More THISday

Join me in the Conversation:

Questions, Thoughts & Comments?

Write to:

philip@philipgabbard.com

Author Bio/Signed Books/Blog/Swag/Journals

Visit:

www.THISday365.com

Follow THISday:

Instagram: @THISday365

Facebook: @THISday365

Twitter: @THISday365247

Spotify: THISday

I invite you to please make inspirational song and lyric suggestions, and please support songwriters, poets, artists, and dreamers! Tell them how their art makes you feel. Give them your words of THISday.

9 781627 877817